T5-CCX-021

LEADERSHIP

IS

EVERYBODY'S

BUSINESS

John D. Lawson, Ed. D.

Leslie J. Griffin, M.A.

Franklyn D. Donant, M.A.

Illustrated by the Bob Clampett Studios

Impact Publishers

POST OFFICE BOX 1094

SAN LUIS OBISPO, CALIFORNIA 93406

First Edition, September, 1976
Third Printing, January 1980

Copyright © 1976
by John D. Lawson, Leslie J. Griffin, and Franklyn D. Donant

All rights reserved under International and Pan-American Copyright Conventions. No part of this book may be reproduced, stored in a retrieval system, or transmitted in any form or by any means, electronic, mechanical, photocopying, recording or otherwise, without express written permission of the authors, except for brief quotations in critical reviews or for quotations from other sources. The authors and publisher gratefully acknowledge permission of those noted in the text for use herein of materials from other publications.

International Standard Book Number: 0-915166-25-9 (Paper)
0-915166-26-7 (Cloth)
Library of Congress Catalog Card Number: 76-026303

Published by ***Impact Publishers***
POST OFFICE BOX 1094
SAN LUIS OBISPO, CALIFORNIA 93406

Printed in the United States of America

Table of Contents

Part II

Part III

This book is for you
And you'll like it a lot
If you care more about people
Than about the title you've got!

PREFACE:

Why Leadership
Is Everybody's Business

This book is for everybody, for all of us. It is meant to help anyone who, as a member of an organization, has been involved in a directionless discussion, a flakey decision, a meaningless project, or an ambiguous position of leadership. It has something for those members of a club or committee who have experienced frustration because the officers dominate the affairs of the organization without involving them. And it is written for the officers of volunteer organizations who make their very best efforts and still wonder why attendance is dropping or why once-active members are apathetic.

Still not sure this book is for you? Well, perhaps some examples will help you decide.

The Fable of the Flakey Decision

It was late, and the P.T.A. meeting had already lasted an hour and a half instead of the promised hour. Everybody was tired, and a little angry that they were still there (they **did** have to get up and go to work the next day, you know). They'd suffered through corrections to the minutes, officers' reports, a discussion of what size emblem to buy for their jackets, and a tirade by the refreshments chairperson who was "sick and tired of being the only one who stayed to clean up after the meetings." People were starting to casually drift away when the president asked for the treasurer's report. (No biggie, right?—wrong!) There was only $12.32 left in the organizational coffers: the treasurer had been on vacation for a month and wanted to know where all the money had gone. And how did they expect to finance the annual dinner-dance that was scheduled for early the next month? (By this time, only the president, the treasurer, and five stalwart members remained from the original group of 35.) No one knew that the vice president (who had been the acting treasurer during the previous month) had collected over $300 in outstanding dues, hid it in his sock in his underwear drawer at home for safe-keeping and forgotten to enter the income in the official books. Frustrated, confused and desperate, the seven people who were still around cancelled the dinner-dance, dissolved the planning committee and went home. No one bothered to give the vice-president a call, and no one had a true picture of the financial situation. They didn't find out about the V.P.'s oversight until two weeks later, when it was too late to reschedule the dinner-dance. In brief, a few people with limited knowledge acted too quickly.

Sound familiar? Read on . . .

The Story of Tessie Who Tired of Trying

Tessie was responsible for all the fund-raising efforts of the local chapter of N.O.W. (National Organization for Women). She believed strongly in the purposes of her organization, and when she first accepted the position three months before, she was full of enthusiasm and hope. Tessie started with a committee of six women who had promised to help her but it seemed that lately each of them had more and more excuses for not attending fund-raising planning meetings. And when they **did** meet, the conversation always drifted to topics other than the financial needs of the organization (job discrimination, the plight of the single mother, the latest book on feminism, etc.). After six months of trying, Tessie quietly submitted her resignation and disappeared. No one really knew why; no one tried to find out.

One more . . .

James: "The People's Choice"

When everybody else declined the nomination, James was left. He was "unanimously" elected president of the Black Students Union, even though he had only been a member of the organization for two months and nobody really knew him very well. John was the group's first choice but he was too busy with community projects to want to assume additional responsibility, and Sarah would have been better than James but she was swamped with school work this semester. So . . . James was electeᴗ president, John ended up being the secretary, and Sarah became the new vice president. Since most members had been in the B.S.U. for a couple of years and knew the organizational ropes, they continued to go to John and Sarah for advice and action, almost as though James didn't exist.   Hurt and frustrated, James started demanding that he be involved in **every** decision that was being made, no matter how trivial. The members responded quickly and decisively: they simply refused to pay their dues until James stepped down or backed off. It was an extremely sensitive situation . . .

Why This Book?

These examples are typical of the problems encountered by many volunteer task-oriented groups that exist today in our communities, our schools, and our colleges and universities. By **volunteer task-oriented groups** we mean any organization or club (like yours?) that has specific purposes, goals or activities, and needs **volunteers** to accomplish the necessary **tasks**. The three of us have worked with many such groups: Girl Scouts, Boy Scouts, Young Farmers, sororities, fraternities, P.T.A.'s, faculty committees, statewide educational committees, junior high "Y" groups, service clubs, community crisis centers, state agricultural organizations, and all manner of college student clubs and committees. And whether we have been involved with these groups as participants, advisors or special consultants, we've been asked to respond to the same kinds of concerns over and over again. For example:

"Why is it that I can't get **anyone** to volunteer for my committee?."

"Why do we officers have to do **all** the work?"

"Why do new members come once or twice and then disappear?"

"Everybody seemed to really like this project last year; why aren't they enthusiastic about it now?"

"Why don't more people ask questions or participate in meetings? They all sit around like they're just waiting for refreshments!"

"**Those** people seem to keep to themselves all the time—don't they want to 'lower' themselves enough to mix with the rest of us?"

"The 'big shot' leaders are always ramming projects down our throats—why don't they let us decide what **we** want to do for a change?"

As a result of teaching classes and conducting workshops on group process, human relations and leadership over a combined total of 30 years, we have realized the need for a book that combines group dynamics theory, philosophy, exercises and resources in such a way that both officers and members can begin to understand what causes some groups to fall apart, what structured experiences will help a group begin to put itself back together again, and where to turn for more detailed information and help.

In a way this book is not only our gift to everybody who has struggled to discover the whys of "task-oriented-groups-with-the-blahs," it is also our gift to each other. Our approach is **humanistic** in that we stress the importance of having a genuine understanding of and respect for the private dynamics of the individual member faced with the process of the group; it is **pragmatic** because we are concerned with what works; and it is **eclectic**, since we draw upon references and techniques that have been used successfully in business, counseling, education and psychology. We have made a sincere effort toward clarity and conciseness so that all readers will find this guide understandable and useful.

Who Will Find This Book Useful?

Task-oriented groups with volunteer memberships exist everywhere. They include people of all ages who are associated with schools, churches, community agencies, service clubs, fraternal orders, trade unions or the professions. Some of these groups are local and involve few external relationships; others are international, with complicated structures tying them together. Some are new—even formative—and without a clear mission or specific objectives. Still others are enriched by or burdened with a legacy of traditions, rituals and alumni. Some are small, others large; some informal and others rigid with procedures—and, to be sure, there is everything in between. But even with these variations, all groups have one thing in common: they are made up of people . . . people with unique needs, feelings, ideas and aspirations.

The people who make up the rank-and-file membership of an organization bring with them special talents: Frank may be the kind of person other members go to with their private concerns, Steve is a terrific organizer and leader, Liz may be a whiz with finances, Al the perfect host and Christie the loyal, dependable behind-the-scenes trooper.

We believe that the material we've compiled will be useful to all of these "unique people," and that the application of a few basic principles of group dynamics will contribute to a happier and more productive group. Furthermore, many of the processes and experiences we offer will have some, if limited, application to non-volunteer groups: families, large institutions, and employees of small and large businesses.

Organization or Group?

Early in the process of putting this book together, we had to make a decision about whether to be totally correct in our

repeated use of the words **organization** and **group** or whether to
address the distinction between the two early in the book and
then use them interchangeably. We have, for the sake of style,
chosen to do the latter, and a brief explanation of these two
terms follows.

A **group** is an assemblage of interacting persons with a
common purpose forming a cluster or unit. Group members
relate to one another informally and without the structure of
elected or designated leaders who have specific roles and
expectations. Whatever structure a group may have is
determined solely by the action of members. Groups may be
formed to discuss a common concern or interest, to study, to
develop self-understanding or competencies, to pray or
meditate, to have a neighborhood party or to survive in the
streets.

An **organization**, on the other hand, is a group wherein
members have differentiated responsibilities in relation to
common goals. The distribution of responsibilities is generally
made clear in such documents as constitutions, bylaws or
standing rules. Organizations are known for having common
goals and objectives, officers, committees, elections, treasuries
and rules of order for making decisions or taking action.

Groups often develop informally within organizations, and
groups may become organizations when the development of this
more formal structure shows promise of better meeting the
needs of the group members.

The focus of this book is on organizations or, to be more exact,
on organizations composed of volunteer members; that is, we
are addressing ourselves to organizations consisting of people
who have the freedom to make decisions for themselves. Such
decisions include electing their own officers and choosing to
terminate their affiliation whenever the disadvantages of
membership outweigh the advantages . . . as **they** see it.

Now that we've made this fundamental distinction, feel free to
read "organization" as "group," and "group" as "organization."

Take It From The Top!

With modern novels, cookbooks or poetry anthologies it may not matter much whether you start in the middle and read backward or start at the back and read forward. We suggest, however, that you begin **this** book at the beginning and read it straight through to the end (an old-fashioned notion, but nonetheless sound).

The material is arranged to take you through all phases of group life, in logical progression. Here's a quick summary of what you have in store.

Part I: The information you'll find in Part I is left out of most the leadership books we've seen, since the primary focus is on the **preliminaries** of leadership.

Chapter 1 explores the general concept of leisure: what people do with their free time, and what factors influence their decision to begin to look for a group to join.

Chapter 2 explains the difference between what it means to be a joiner and what it means to be a member. This distinction isn't often discussed, but we feel it's a significant one.

Be sure to **read Chapter 3 carefully**. This is where you'll find some practical suggestions about how to welcome new members into your group, how to make them feel at home, and how to get people acquainted so that they'll be ready to begin working on group tasks. These techniques are an essential part of effective leadership, and if they are done well, group morale will be strong and production will be high.

Don't ignore the humanness of your membership; it's organizational suicide if you do.

Part II: This is a **must** for all leaders, whether brand new or experienced. We view this section of the book as a handbook of necessary organizational skills or competencies; it includes things every leader should know how to do. Leaders who master the skills contained in each of these seven chapters will be well on their way to "success"; leaders who don't master these skills will be fighting an uphill battle all the way. Which would you rather do?

Part III: If you're concerned about some of the "finer points" of organizational dynamics, Part III will be especially interesting for you. The five chapters go beyond what is basic to good leadership and explore some essential (though more advanced) concepts: the cycle of organizational involvement (Chapter 11); how **your** actions affect others (Chapter 12); the dynamics of role conflicts among group members (Chapter 13); and what you can do to improve individual motivation and communication among your members (Chapter 14).

In **Chapter 11** you'll find that there are specific "phases" a person passes through during the time he or she is involved with an organization. Since this cycle of organizational involvement affects the operations of the organization, we believe it will help both new and continuing leaders to better understand what's happening.

Chapter 12 describes five general leadership styles, and explores the many ways in which each of these styles has a predictable impact on group processes.

In **Chapter 13** role conflict is defined in some detail, and we offer some concrete suggestions for overcoming its negative effects.

Chapter 14 deals with the basic concepts of motivation and inter-personal communications. Along with a discussion of what you can do to enhance motivation are references to exercises you can use to improve the quality of group communications.

Chapter 15 deals with the practical application of many of the concepts we've discussed throughout the book. It's really a summing up of suggestions for action we think will be helpful to you in day-to-day leadership situations.

There you have it: a little symphony of leadership for you to perform. Take it from the top, Maestro!

PART I

INTRODUCTION:

Leadership Is . . .
Being Human

In Part I our primary focus will be on the individual: his or her values, motivation for joining groups, and ability to make others feel comfortable in an organizational setting. These three chapters contain information and ideas often omitted from books on leadership, since the concepts presented are **not** what many would call "hard core" leadership skills. Still, we believe that it is having a solid understanding of these leadership preliminaries that very often makes the difference between so-so groups and great ones. For example:

In **Chapter 1** we discuss the topic of leisure, and stress the importance of realizing that needs and values play a tremendous role in an individual's choice of a voluntary group (as well as in determining the degree and length of his or her association with it). We offer an exercise that will help you get in better touch with what **your** needs, values and possible leisure options are, and suggest that this activity can also be used to clarify the needs and values of members in an already established group. The reason we've devoted an entire chapter to needs and values is that we believe it's essential for organizational leaders to give some thought to whether or not their **group** needs and values reflect (or are compatible with) those of the current membership. The match doesn't have to be perfect, but if you find that there is a substantial difference between the two, it may be a clue as to why the members are not as involved or enthusiastic as you would like them to be.

Chapter 2 is devoted to a discussion of the distinction between "joiner and member." Most organizations are made up of a combination of both kinds of people (indeed, both are often needed to accomplish group goals). It's important, nonetheless, to recognize that a joiner has a different level of commitment to the organization than a member does, and in order to keep both interested in the activities and projects of the group, leaders' expectations of each should differ. Joiners should not be forced into accepting too much responsibility too fast, and members should be continuously challenged by being given greater and greater responsibility in organizational affairs.

In **Chapter 3** we share some easily-executed group activities that we've found helpful in making new members feel welcome; we also give ways to alleviate stereotyping and ways to be aware of the first impressions formed among members. There are eight practical exercises at the end of the chapter that can be used by **any** organizational leader to accomplish these purposes and none requires an expert presentation to be effective. Getting group members acquainted with one another before the real work of the organization begins is **extremely** important, and too often it's not done well (for no other reason than many leaders simply don't know how to do it). Chapter 3 is one of the most important chapters in the entire book, the time you spend with it will be worthwhile.

Part I begins at the beginning of organizational involvement and positive group dynamics. It's the foundation you'll need to build within your group the strong interpersonal relationships that are so necessary for cohesive action and mutual understanding.

Want a glimpse of people's dreams?
A hint of what they long for?
A man at leisure soon reveals
The things he's right or wrong for.

CHAPTER 1

Leisureship . . . Time for You!

"You can't eat for eight hours a day nor drink for eight hours a day nor make love for eight hours a day . . . all you can do for eight hours a day is work. Which is the reason why man makes himself and everybody else so miserable and unhappy." [1]

Why is it that so many of our job-related experiences are not fully satisfying? It's mostly because the conditions of employment limit the amount of freedom we have to do things of our own choosing, in our own way and at our own pace. On the job there are policies, supervisors, customers, clients, deadlines, job descriptions and regular financial obligations to keep us in line, hampering our autonomy. Whatever the nature of our work, or training and education for work, it **does** place constraints upon what we do, as well as how and when we do it. Most of us must work at some sort of job for our daily bread. And gainful employment also gives us the means to "buy ourselves" some free time, some leisure to enjoy when the day's work is done or schooling is over.

Freedom is the essence of leisure; learning how to use your freedom is the key to maximum personal fulfillment. To say that what you do in your personal free time is more fulfilling,

---

1. Faulkner, William, in Preface of the book *Working*, by Studs Terkel, New York: Pantheon Books, Division of Random House, Inc., 1975. Used with permission.

spontaneous and innovative than what you do at work or while being schooled for work may be too sweeping a statement to make categorically; you may find your work (or schooling) both stimulating and satisfying. There is a different frame of reference for leisure than for work: in your spare time the focus is likely to be "me," at work or school your concerns must often be with "it" or "they."

Your leisure experiences can be beautiful or ugly, creative or tedious, meaningful or useless, joyful or painful. The alternatives you have—to grow, to create and to seek what will satisfy you—are limited only by lack of knowledge or understanding of what you like to do (your own needs and values), or by limited awareness of the self-fulfilling opportunities available in your environment.

In the remainder of this chapter, then, we will discuss ways of finding out what your real needs and values are. We'll also touch on the impact needs and values have on the decisions people make about choosing volunteer task-oriented groups to join.

One of the main reasons we have devoted the first chapter of our book on leadership to the topic of leisure and group choice is that both are important concepts for leaders to understand. If you don't know **how** people make these kinds of decisions, you won't have the opportunity to influence them.

Throughout this next section imagine that you are an enthusiastic, prospective group member. How can you go about selecting activities that have some promise of meeting your needs?

First, you must become aware of what those needs are and discover which of your personal priorities take precedence over others.

EXERCISE I: THE LIVING NAME TAG[2]

The Living Name Tag is one way to learn more about yourself; it provides a relatively non-threatening opportunity to "zero in" on

---

2. Ideas and exercise acquired from and used with permission of Marianne Simon, University of Massachusetts. Adapted from seminar presentation, 1975 Association of College Unions—International Conference, Hollywood, Florida.

how you perceive yourself and the world around you. It can be used in a group situation, too, as a means of getting to know more about the values and needs of others in your organization. We believe that the Living Name Tag is only a beginning; perhaps it will simply give you a chance to pause long enough to assess what's important to you *right now*, and then (if you choose) you can share your discoveries with others.

The instructions for the Living Name Tag are directed toward use in a group. If you'd rather just use it privately to discover more about *your* personal priorities, simply read the 10 questions, write down your answers, and think about them. We think it will be an enlightening experience for you and may tell you some things that will help you to better understand the direct connection between your values and how you choose to spend your leisure time.

I. Introductory Instructions to the Group

If you've never had a group activity like this during a meeting, your instructions should be given in such a way that people will want to participate fully, not be frightened away. We suggest that the introduction go something like this:

"Now that we've been meeting together for a couple of weeks, your executive committee and I thought it might be interesting for all of us to get to know each other a little better. We have an activity called "Living Name Tag" that we think will make this possible, and we hope you'll want to join in. It involves nothing more than sharing a little bit of yourself—things you like and value—with two or three others in the group, or you can choose to share nothing at all if that's better for you. We have the supplies all prepared; and we'll tell you how to proceed in a minute, but before we get started, are there any questions?"

II. Supplies

1. A 5" x 8" index card and pen or pencil for each participant.
2. A stop watch or watch with a second hand.

III. Creating the Name Tag

Once you've given an index card to each person, instruct them as follows:

"Now . . . we're going to ask that you respond to 10 different questions and that you print your response in a particular place on your card; we'll tell you where as we go along. Everybody ready? Let's go."

Since the spacing of responses is critical, you may want to put the numerical layout of the name tag on a chalkboard or easel. It looks like this:

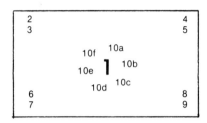

Question 1: "What's your name? Please put your answer in the middle of your card in fairly large letters, but no bigger than about an inch."

Question 2: "What's the name of the place where you spent the three happiest days of your life? . . . Make sure that you answer with a place where you were happy three days *in a row.* Put your answer way up in the top left-hand corner of your card."

Question 3: "This answer will go right underneath the last one, up in the left-hand corner. Where do you most often go when you want to be alone—do you have a special thinking place?"

Question 4: "Up in the top right-hand corner, please write your answer to the following question: Who is someone, whether living or dead, fictitious or real, met or unmet, that you *really* respect or admire (other than members of your immediate family)?"

Question 5: "Your answer to Question 5 goes right below your response to Question 4, up in the right-hand corner. Who is the person in your life that brings you happiness or joy—makes you smile—almost every time you see him or her?"

Question 6: "Your response to Question 6 will go down in the lower left-hand corner of your card, but leave enough space below it to put the answer to Question 7, too. The question is: When you make decisions, in what order do you do these three things:

think—feel—act? That is, do you act before you think or feel? Do you feel before you act and think, or what? Please put them in the order that is most often true of the way you make decisions."

Question 7: "Let me preface this question by acknowledging that we all define *love* in our own ways and in many different ways; using *your* own definition, what are the names of three men you love and those of three women you love? These answers go at the very bottom of the left-hand corner of your card, right under your answer to Question 6."

Question 8: "The answer to Question 8 goes in the space just opposite your response to Question 6; a little bit up from the bottom of your card, but in the lower right-hand corner. Here's the question: During what *year* did you experience the greatest amount of personal growth; that is, what year was most significant in terms of your own development? You can put a single year if you want, like 1965, or you can put something like 1971-1972."

Question 9: "Now, this question's a little tougher, since it deals with death, a topic most of us prefer not to dwell upon. And there are different kinds of death: spiritual, emotional, physical. The answer to this one, though, goes in the lower right-hand corner of your card, right under your response to Question 8. Ready? What was the year *you* came closest to death? Again, define death in your own way—it can mean different things to different people."

Question 10: "The answers to Question 10, the last question we'll ask, should be written in a circle around your name, in the middle of the card. Here's your chance to make yourself feel good. What are six things about yourself that you're proud of; what can you do well that makes you feel kind of special?" We'll give you a few minutes to go back and think about your answers or fill in some you may have omitted the first time around. Does anyone want a question repeated?"

IV. Forming Groups

Once everyone has finished writing their answers, ask them to form groups of three. Stress that it will be a more meaningful experience if they get in a group with people they know very little about (avoid groupings of close friends).

V. Sharing the Name Tags

Explain that each participant will be given *only three minutes* to share any, all, or none of his or her name tag with the other two people in the group. The other two people *cannot respond verbally*; instead they must, through non-verbal communication, listen, empathize, encourage and respond. Call "time" at the end of each three-minute period.

VI. Feedback

Once all three group participants have had a chance to share their name tags, give the groups approximately 10 minutes to respond to one another verbally. Suggest that group members begin their feedback with "I liked it when you said . . . "

VII. Discussion

Once the exercise has been completed, a discussion of member reactions to the activity will be helpful. Here are some questions you might want to ask to stimulate interaction:
- Did any of you learn anything new about yourselves that you hadn't known before?
- Do you see any connection between your answers to these questions and your values?
- Did you find that you had many *possible* responses and that it was difficult to choose just one?
- Were there some questions you didn't want to answer?
- Were there some answers you didn't want to share with others in your group? Why?
- During feedback, was it difficult to give a compliment and/or receive one? Why?

If you can come up with some better questions—ones that may be more appropriate for your particular group—feel free to use them. These are only suggestions.

VIII. Helpful Hints

We believe that the Living Name Tag can be used with any group whose members are high-school age and over. There are a couple of things you might keep in mind, though, that will make your first experience with it more satisfying:

1. Don't make the decision to use this activity without consulting your group's officers *first* about its appropriateness. And, since most people don't like to have something like this "sprung" on them, it might be wise to announce a meeting ahead of time: "Next week we're planning to do something that will get us all better acquainted. We hope to see you here."

2. Make sure participants understand that they can choose not to answer any question, at any time, and that they need not share everything they write down. The real point of the name tag is *self* awareness, *personal* values clarification; *under no circumstances* should people be forced to reveal their answers against their wills.

3. Be sure to allow ample time after reading each question for participants to write down their answers. Even if you give them three or four minutes for each one, the exercise can still be done within an hour's time.

4. If you think some of the questions are too personal for your group, change them to meet organizational needs. For example, instead of the "death" question, you may want to substitute "What's the name of the organization that you've belonged to that has brought you the most joy?" Or instead of the "love" question, perhaps: "What are activities you'd like to have this group sponsor this year?" No matter what the questions, the process remains the same.

What the living name tag is all about is identifying those activities that may enhance personal growth, well-being and happiness. The ultimate goal of values clarification (as exemplified by the Living Name Tag) is to sort out "what counts"; the process requires dedication and, from time to time, support and help from close friends. Becoming aware of values is an exercise in being honest with yourself (and others). It is necessary to determine what your values are before it is possible to assess realistically whether or not this group or that group will expand or limit the meaningfulness of your leisure experiences.

The Dynamics of Actually Choosing a Group

Once you begin to discover and understand those things that

have brought you joy in the past, the next decision you must make is whether to pursue similar activities alone or in the company of others, now or in the future. If you choose the former, the helpfulness of our book ends here. But if you opt to share your time with others (as most of us do) you can begin to probe your environment for information about groups that might be appealing to you. (While you cannot deny the impact of past experiences on your decisions, neither should you allow yourself to become bogged down or limited by them. Choosing only those activities which are familiar or sure will restrict you severely in considering all **possible** leisure pursuits.)

During this process you should check carefully to see if the values of the group are compatible with yours, and if the activities of the group show some promise of fulfilling your needs. Also, it would be wise to determine where each group is positioned on the continuum of individual freedom and constraints, for even volunteer organizations vary greatly in this respect. As a prospective member you need to find out about the purposes and goals and limitations of groups and what will be expected of you **before** you accept membership.

It is our contention that the most successful groups are made up of members who know their individual preferences in advance and who have a realistic notion of the group's purposes and constraints. Such organizations have great promise: not only can they meet the needs of the members; they can also accomplish goals. The members are optimistic and their expectations are high. In short, these are **leisure groups** in the best sense of the word.

The Art of Leisureship

We have spent quite a bit of time emphasizing the important role that leisureship plays in enhancing personal growth. But before you dive headlong into hastily-chosen or "too many" group activities, take heed.

Sometimes your decision to join a particular group will be more inspired from "without" than from "within." The pressure and demands to conform often put on you by your peers may threaten to destroy whatever enjoyment you might find during your valuable moments of freedom. Being accepted by individuals and groups is a need we all have, but acceptance at what cost? Beware of taking up a leisure activity just because you think you "ought to"; try to limit yourself to joining groups because you "want to." It's not only **appropriate**, it's often **necessary** to be selfish when it comes to getting the greatest enjoyment from your all-too-few moments of freedom.

Over indulgence, too, is risky. The novelty of something new can stimulate your interest and involvement; this is as true of joining groups as it is of eating too much of the "specialty of the house." An organizational "overdose" can result in a temporary misordering of your priorities, or in just plain dropping out from exhaustion. You can do just so much with your time. It's easy to take on too much; you will probably come away disenchanted and overworked rather than joyful. Certainly, some in the group will encourage your zealousness, and perhaps even take unfair advantage of it. Enthusiasm and commitment are one thing—but "o.d.ing" on groups can lead to personal tragedy.

The choice of leisure activities is often a more complex process than it appears to be. In order to make a wise decision, you should take several factors into consideration:

- What **are** your personal needs and values?
- Are the values of the group(s) you are considering compatible with yours?
- Do the activities of the group(s) show promise of meeting your needs?
- Will the group(s) allow you enough freedom?
- Are the goals of the group(s) ones that you would like to help achieve?

Review each of these factors; they are basic to the next step, relating to the perceptions of new members, which we'll explore in greater depth in Chapters 2 and 3.

If you're troubled when members
Give nothing but dues,
Check things they believe in
For gut-level clues.

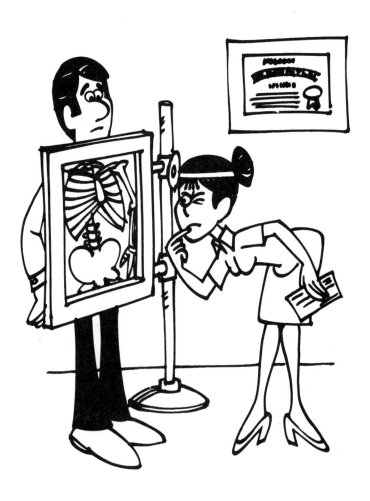

CHAPTER 2

Joiners & Members:
Attitudes, Values, Behaviors

What does it really mean to be a member of a group? Is it paying dues? Is it attending meetings? Is it signing a roll sheet? Is it wearing "the pin"? Is it carrying a card? Is it knowing a password? Is it attending the functions of the organization? Some will say, "If he is willing to do all that, of course he is a member of our group." Let's probe a little deeper.

Membership cards, titles, pins and the like may create status for an individual but they do not necessarily represent a gut-level investment of the personal self. This is what separates the "joiners" from the "members." Those groups who base their membership goals on the number of card-holders or dues-payers they have are likely to be on the road to apathy and limited achievement. An organization with a disproportional number of "joiners" has increased the chances that the members will form splinter groups or cliques to redefine their needs, carry on in other directions, or (more seriously) dissolve the organization entirely.

Examples of "joiner mania" aren't hard to find. Recently a district council of the Boy Scouts of America found itself wrapped up in a minor scandal. Feeling pressure from the national organization to keep pace with the required quotas, the local district padded its membership list with a few extra names. Obviously, having a bunch of fictitious members hanging around doesn't hold much promise for the future of the organization, especially when the original goals of the organization are subverted for the sake of numbers.

A "joiner" is, essentially, an undeveloped member.

Being a **member** requires taking positive action (or constructive action) within the organization. Being a **member** involves a personal, gut-level identification with and acceptance of the realities of the group. Being a **member** means accepting and identifying with the organization's goals and objectives, its programs, its values and philosophy, and its collective personality. Being a **member** also means being yourself and maintaining your individuality as you relate to other people in the group as well as to the group as a whole. It's not necessarily an easy road to travel, but if you've been honest with yourself in defining your needs and the group has been honest with you in communicating its purposes, you will be a **member** rather than a joiner.

Perhaps an illustration will make this distinction more understandable. Clay and Lisa were both affiliated with the community church guild. They were both considered to be model citizens of the community, involved with church happenings, and present at all church functions. But those who worked closely with them knew the similarities between the two really stopped there.

Lisa attended all guild meetings and was an integral part of the decision-making and goal-setting processes of the organization. She was committed to the guild's goals of providing support, education and entertainment for the church congregation. Although she had enough enthusiasm for 10 people, she managed to create an atmosphere of team work among the other people in the guild, realizing and appreciating how necessary each individual was to the success of the organization.

Clay by no means lacked the moral qualities which had won him a great deal of esteem and popularity in the community. He enjoyed the programs and activities the guild provided and, as a result, was usually in attendance at the guild meetings. He contributed to discussions but rarely volunteered any extra time to the organization. It was important for him to be involved with the church, for the social and political benefits which the church provided him and his family were an important part of his personal life style.

The chart that follows will help to point out this subtle (yet significant) difference in the relationship between joiners and members of an organization. All volunteer task-oriented groups will have both members and joiners in them; our point here is that the attitudes, values and behaviors of each will have different effects on the organization.

As is indicated in the chart, it's often possible to distinguish a joiner from a member simply by paying attention to the way a person **talks** about the organization; the words he or she uses may give you a clue to his or her level of involvement. A common example of this can be found in the use of the words "we" and "they."

Laura, a member of the finance committee for over a year, became frustrated when she attempted to explain the decisions this committee had made. "**They** didn't appropriate the money you requested," she explained. (She constantly referred to the decisions **they** had made.) When she was made aware of what she had said, she admitted that she had never really felt like a member of the finance committee. Her use of the word "they" rather than "we" in discussing the committee's decisions "gave away" her honest feelings about the degree to which she identified with that group.

The **key** to all this is that a **member** (in the true sense of the word) makes definite commitments to the organization. These commitments are identifiable behaviorally: whereas a **joiner** may be an expert at lip service, a **member** will carry verbal commitments into action. A **joiner** will generally try to impress you with his or her title, pin, card or surface dedication to an organization, but a member is more concerned with actual fellowship and achievement of goals, and will not hesitate publicly to defend or support the organization. There is harmony between the **member's** needs, values and philosophy and those of the organization.

THE DIFFERENCE BETWEEN JOINERS AND MEMBERS

	JOINERS	MEMBERS
	Enjoyment	**Participation**
Primary reason for belonging to the group	Joiners are really interested in the "fun" aspects of organizational life. They will probably attend meetings and social events regularly, but will seldom serve on committees or volunteer to do necessary (though unexciting) tasks.	Members keep their promises to the organization and do their "fair share" of the work. They will participate actively in setting goals and achieving them, will serve on committees and run for office. Through their active involvement, they become committed.
	"Me" Orientation	**"We" Orientation**
General relationship to the group	Joiners are concerned about what the group can do for them. They will give their financial support freely if they receive certain benefits in return: social status, recognition, a feeling of importance. Their main objective in affiliation is not to help, but to be helped.	Members anticipate that the group will meet some of their needs, but they will contribute their **time** as well as their money. Material or public benefits are secondary to them; they feel a "Gutlevel" involvement with group purposes. They will not hesitate to defend the organization in the face of criticism or attack.
	Low/Selective/Short-Term	**High/General/Long-Term**
Level of involvement	Joiners tend to appear only when the task appeals to them. They may pay their dues at the beginning of the year just so they can participate in one or two events. Their involvement is based on immediate need-fulfillment and changing interests. They are somewhat fickle about their participation and involvement.	Members will support **all** group tasks, either directly or indirectly. They keep the purpose and long-term goals of the organization in mind, and lend year-after-year continuity to the group. They are willing to forego short-term pleasure or fun in the interest of long-term progress or accomplishment.
	Lack of Identification	**Strong Identification**
Some things these people might say	"Hey—when are they going to bring out the refreshments?!" "I'd really **like** to help, but I just have too many other things to do." "I think a talent show is a **great** idea—I'll make a perfect M.C." "Let's just have the same kind of B-B-Q as last year—it was fun!"	"The refreshments are coming, but we still have some important decisions to make tonight." "Well, if you really need help, I'll be there." "Let's spend some time brainstorming some **new** program ideas." "According to the financial report, the B-B-Q didn't do very well. How can we make it better?"

	JOINERS	MEMBERS
	Don't Expect Too Much	**Provide Challenge & Opportunity**
How should the organization respond?	Joiners are needed in every organization. They help out financially, and they're enthusiastic about projects that interest them. Treat them with respect, but don't force them to accept too much responsibility—you might scare them away. Give them special things to do that they'll enjoy.	Members are willing to work and work hard, but they need to have new challenges that will give them a feeling of accomplishment. Just because a member does something well, don't keep him or her doing it year after year. These people are your organization's most valuable resources; don't exhaust them!

Joining a group is simple—but becoming a **member** is a total experience. And since leisure organizations can't be all things to all people, the challenge is to find one or two organizations which are in harmony with you. Only then will true MEMBERSHIP be yours.

In Chapter 3, we'll expand the concept of membership and discuss some group activities that can be used by your organization to convert some of your joiners into members. Most of them involve little more than getting people acquainted with one another, but this is a crucial step in the process of transforming the individual feelings of "me" into the more productive "we".

The world can be a lonely place
If looks are all you go on;
So take some time and get to know
What other people grow on.

CHAPTER 3

First Impressions:
Preparing New Members

You walk into the meeting room. There are about 25 strangers standing around, talking casually. Up near the front there are a few people who seem to be in charge. Without warning, the conversation stops, and all eyes turn to you, "the newcomer!" Awful silence descends. You squelch the impulse to turn and bolt for the door. At last—long last— someone comes up to you and extends his hand, "Hi." (Thank God!)

Everyone who has ever made the decision to attend a meeting of a group in which all the members are unknown to him or her has had an experience similar to this one. All too often the scene develops in church youth groups, Senior Citizen's centers, Rotary Club luncheons, Boy Scout meetings, and during open rush at fraternity houses. It also occurs when a person moves into a new community, changes schools, or goes to college as a freshman or transfer student. Let's go back and look more closely at the dynamics of the situation.

First of all, it's important to realize that whenever two strangers encounter one another for the first time, first impressions are formed. This is something we're all aware of, but the complexity of forming first impressions is tremendous, and it increases with the number of people present.

What is this phenomenon of first impressions all about? What is it that causes people to make judgments about others on the basis of a few seconds' interaction with them? What can be done to prevent the perpetuation of first impressions within a group? The answers to these questions have important implications for all organizations. The effects that persisting first impressions can have are numerous: role conflicts can develop, quality decisions can be prevented, communications can break down, cliques can be formed, and group consensus can be nonexistent. First impressions should not be taken lightly; they need to be dealt with in an understanding and sensitive manner.

For example: When I meet you (assuming we're strangers), there are two impressions being formed—mine of you and yours of me. Seems simple enough, right? Wrong! Increase the number to 25 (a number that is not unrealistic at the first meeting of a new group); in this instance, if all the people in the room are strangers to one another, **600** first impressions will be formed. (If you're interested in figuring out how many may be forming at your meetings, you can compute it by using the formula $x = (n-1)n$, in which x = the number of first impressions and n = the number of people present who don't know each other.)

Whether the group is as large as 25, or as small as two, within a few seconds (or at the longest a few minutes) people make emotionally-based and surprisingly **lasting** decisions about which people they would probably like to get to know better and which people they would just as soon keep at a distance. Imagine—600 impressions may be forming all at once—transactions that can have tremendous impact on the future of the group!

How First Impressions Are Formed

Most of us crave familiarity and commonality and have a general fear of the unknown. Thus, the old saying really does ring true: "Birds of a feather flock together," (and "lotsa luck" to those who seem different on first sight). How do we establish familiarity during a brief meeting with another person?

The most obvious way is by assessing a person's general attitude on the basis of his or her physical features and clothing—you can tell something about people by the way they look. You do this all the time: on the street, in the supermarket, on the job, at school and throughout organizational life. You "check out" each other. Does Bill stand straight or stooped, is Tina dirty or clean, is Jana's hair styled or natural, is Larry's skin black or white, is Pam neat or sloppy, are Bob's clothes cheap or expensive, or is Eunice fat or skinny? All these things that contribute to a person's appearance are potential clues to his profession, her political leanings, and your feelings about whether or not similarity exists between you. In short, they help you determine how much like you the other person might be. And, chances are, the more he looks like you, the more you will be attracted to him or her. Why? Because surprises are unwelcome (and a little frightening) in new relationships, and we feel more comfortable with someone whose behavior is somewhat predictable.

Beyond physical appearances, there are other criteria we use to form our initial impressions of another person. These include:

• His or her manner of speech—accents, colloquialisms (hip vs. square usage), tone of voice, rapidity of speech, regional peculiarities, etc.

• Who the person "hangs around with"—personal friends, who he or she came to the meeting with, sits down next to, etc.

• What others have said about the person prior to the meeting (or, in the case of an influential individual, what you have read about the person).

• His or her name or title.

There may be more—think about it.

It's important for group leaders to be aware of the processes which are occuring at meetings, especially for newcomers. The group leader should identify each new face and empathize with the newcomer in a spirit of welcome. Without this basic hospitality, the other steps described in this chapter will have little value.

One of the most interesting things about first impressions is that their influence on us does not stop with our "categorizing" of a single individual; they are quickly and subtly expanded so that we can place that individual into a larger reference group: he becomes part of a stereotype.

Stereotypes will vary from culture to culture (and will differ even among some sub-cultures in American society), but there are some that most of us readily recognize. For instance, in the mid- and late sixties, there were lots of young people running around who had long hair, beards, love beads, flowers, sandals, clothes seemingly purchased at Goodwill, and an assortment of dogs. These folks were called "hippies" and it was assumed by many that because of their physical appearance, their speech, their associates, and their collective reputation, they all engaged in identical behavior—they probably smoked dope, belonged to the same political party (if any), were anti-establishment and anti-military, threw rocks in campus riots, and believed in and practiced the "new morality." Further, on the basis of these assumptions, "non-hippies" based their reactions to, attitudes about, and behavior toward this group of people on these stereotyped images.

Although there are many other stereotypes we could discuss (e.g.: "frat rats", southerners, military personnel, movie stars, athletes, librarians, and politicians) this one will serve to make our point, which is: the stereotyping that results from the hasty formation of first impressions negates the reality of individuality and thus is harmful to interpersonal and group relationships, and healthy group dynamics. To be fully functioning, groups must discover the **uniqueness** of each individual member and utilize his or her special personal resources in the accomplishment of tasks and the achievement of goals. Perpetuation of first impressions or allowing stereotypes to persist is counterproductive to the growth of the group and to the fulfillment of its potential.

Team Building

The crux, then, of group productivity and morale is to foster individuality among the membership. This begins by helping the members get to know each other **beyond** the first impression level, and **beyond** the shallow verbal dead end of "name, rank and serial number" (name, class level, major . . . name, profession, family). We give this process a name—**team building**.

The discipline of avoiding the potential impact of first impressions and stereotyping so that it's possible to begin building a team is not easy. It requires empathy, sensitivity and practice. At the end of this chapter are a series of exercises designed to help reduce the tendency to form unchangeable first impressions, especially in situations where newcomers and continuing members are together for the first time. These exercises might also assist an organization that must confront the fact that some personality conflicts or cliques have developed.

Exercise 2, " 'Who Am I?': A Getting-Acquainted Activity", and Exercise 3, " 'Who Am I?' Variation: A Getting-Acquainted Activity"; can help members get acquainted at a first meeting; they are relatively non-threatening, and can be fun.

Exercise 4, "Person-to-Person Name Tags: Sharing Questions and Answers" as well as Exercise 5, "Interviews and Introductions" can also be used at a first meeting. They may, however, be used more appropriately as a means of ongoing, periodic introductions for large organizations, as a part of the agenda for middle-of-the-year meetings, or to improve inter-personal communication and sharing during a workshop or retreat.

None of these exercises require the skills of a trained leader; you need only the desire to get to know other people more genuinely. By using any one (or more) of these, we think you'll discover some surprising things about people you thought you knew pretty well—and you'll simultaneously increase the appreciation of individuality and the concept of "team" within the group.

We realize that there are those who believe that such "getting to know you games" are O.K., but that time pressure is a major factor in group life and usually limits the use of too many morale-related experiences during regular meetings. Making the most productive use of time is crucial to any organization.

However, there are ways to caringly bring new members into your "culture" while still accomplishing tasks.

Preparing New Members for The Rites of Passage

We usually encounter the term "rites of passage" in anthropology or sociology. But our lives are full of examples of such rites or processes which provide a transition from one status to another: birthday parties, promotions in rank, the first prom, receiving a certificate or a degree. Our focus is on the rites of passage that help new members to become part of a group. We have several suggestions which can be incorporated into the functioning of your group or club with good results.

The **first** of these processes, represented by the pledge class, has been used effectively for over a hundred years by honorary, service and social organizations, although it has seldom been adopted by very many other groups for whom it might prove to be very helpful.

Using this approach to "enculturate" new members depends upon having the influx of new members happen at a specific time once (or more) during the year (e.g.: the first meeting after school starts, the first meeting after officer installation, the second Tuesdays in November and April—whenever). Or, your group can establish a cut-off date for a membership drive (e.g.: "All those who join prior to November 20 will be in Pledge Class #1.") The time schedule is secondary; the important thing is to provide the new members with a collective identity in which to demonstrate their individual potential, and for you to recognize that they have special needs to which the existing members should be sensitive.

Once the pledge population has been identified, it is necessary to choose someone to administer the pledge program, and to plan a series of activities that will be meaningful to the new members as well as assist them in becoming productive members of the larger group.

Selecting a Pledge Educator

Most groups that have a pledge program also have a pledge

educator as an elected or appointed officer: a single person whose only organizational responsibility is to pass the group's cultural traits along to the new members. Since your group is entrusting the fate of all its future members to this person, he or she should be among the most dependable, understanding, communicative and participatory of the membership; in short, a model member of the organization, one of whom all the other members are proud.

It is this person the pledges will use as a guide. From the pledge educator they will learn many behaviors and attitudes that will affect group life long into the future. For this reason, the pledge educators should have a solid understanding of the history, goals, structure and membership of the organization; without these they will be unable to communicate the meaning of membership to the pledges and will not be able to transmit the details of the culture to them. If the pledge educator fails in this task, the new members may become old members without really understanding the essential mores and traditions of the group. And if they don't understand them, they can't perpetuate them.

Transmitting the Necessary Information

A big part of any program for new members should include information they will need to participate fully in the activities of the group; in other words, basic facts that will make them feel more comfortable and knowledgeable. Some suggestions are:

- A list of names, addresses and phone numbers of all members and officers.
- A verbal presentation or written history of the group (where and when it began, who the original members were, what awards the group has won, distinguished "alumni," typical activities or projects the group has undertaken in the past, etc.) To do this more effectively, some organizations have created manuals for new members which are updated annually.
- "Do's and don'ts" and traditions that the group feels strongly about—whether they are formally stated or informally understood.

- An explanation of the nitty-gritty mechanics of membership such as how much dues are and when they are to be paid, what special uniforms or equipment—if any—must be purchased, when regular and special meetings are held, and attendance requirements.
- A detailed discussion of the bylaws or constitution (purpose, goals, objectives of the group—an in depth look at why the group exists and the parameters of its operations). As we said in Chapter 1, every group tends to limit the freedom of its members, and it's only fair that all pledges know the extent of any limitation from the outset.

All this information, along with any other tidbits that your group feels are essential to meaningful participation in the life of the group, will begin to transform the unknown into the familiar for the new members, and thus will help them feel more at ease. One of the most significant purposes of "pledgeship" is that it gives the uninitiated the opportunity to learn the ropes in a relatively secure group of their peers, and helps them to be more confident that their actions at group functions, or offers of assistance to the established members will not be viewed as inappropriate or wrong.

Possible Activities for Productivity

In addition to this sharing of factual information, there are many activities that a pledge group can participate in or sponsor that will increase the productivity of the group as a whole. If the members have two projects they want to complete in a given period of time but only have the manpower for one, the second can be turned over entirely to the pledges. Better yet, allow the pledges to determine their own service projects. Pledges can sponsor social functions and invite the entire membership or they can work side by side with the members to accomplish an important task.

Using the pledge class approach to the enculturation of new members simultaneously accomplishes two things: it allows the parent group to continue to work on tasks without untimely interruptions or unnecessary delays, and it makes the new members feel secure, special and participatory. If dealing with and holding new members has been a problem for your group, pledging is worth a try—and the beauty of this approach is that it can be modified (made more or less structured) to meet your unique needs.

Since, in most cases, new members do not know each other very well, and since like continuing members, they might be inclined to form some hasty impressions of fellow new members, we have included two additional exercises at the end of this chapter that can be used to break down interpersonal barriers before they become too well established.

Exercise 6, "Listening and Inferring: A Getting-Acquainted Exercise" is excellent for a newly-formed group such as a pledge class. Because it's non-threatening, it will give new members the opportunity to share a bit of themselves with others. Exercise 7, "First Names, First Impressions: A Feedback Exercise," gets down to the nitty-gritty of new-group first impressions. This exercise clarifies the initial impact that an individual has on other people and also points out how first impressions can affect the group as a whole. We also highly recommend this exercise for organizations that have a strong need to improve interpersonal relationships among the entire membership.

Big and Little Sisters and Brothers

A second technique that can be used to help new members feel welcome is that of pairing each new member with an experienced one—the ol' "Big/Little Brother/Sister" thing (you probably won't want to designate it as such if those terms have negative connotations for the members of your group). This process has been used by a diverse number of organizations such as the Boy Scouts, Alcoholics Anonymous, on-the-job apprentice programs, and the Hare Krishna. It, too, is a means of enculturation, but the responsibility is divided more evenly among the entire membership.

The motivational implications, especially with regard to continuing members, are vast, for, in effect, each old member becomes a pledge educator for a single new member. You may want to allow each new/continuing member to choose someone, or you may want to "buddy people up" based on mutual interests, backgrounds, needs of the new member and skills of the continuing member, or any other criterion that is meaningful to the purposes of your group. With this method, too, each new member has a model and someone to use as a guide in the ways of the group, once again removing that element of fear of the unknown. Still, it is also important to provide each old member with some guidelines that will aid him/her in knowing what information should be given to the new member—otherwise, the experienced member may overlook something that the group feels is important. An added bonus is that experienced members are thus encouraged to renew their acquaintance with the factual foundations of the organization—something they may not do without incentive.

If you employ the Big/Little Brother/Sister format, new members will be spared many of the problems that "solo" newcomers encounter: they don't have to arrive at activities alone, they always have someone to call if they need information or a ride, there's someone to introduce them to other members, and someone to answer questions about group protocol and policies. And, by initiating this kind of program, chances are you'll have twice the number of people showing up to do group projects as was previously the case.

The next to the last exercise we've included in this chapter fits in quite appropriately with organizations that may find the Big/Little Brother/Sister concept more atuned to their needs than the pledge program. Exercise 8, "The Littlest Angel Boxes" is an excellent means of opening up conversations between new and continuing members. You'll get the most mileage out of this exercise if you present it at a pot-luck dinner (or some other low-key event) rather than at a business meeting. This exercise can be helpful, too, as a means of introducing your organization's officers to the total membership at the beginning of the year.

The final exercise in this Chapter is one that can be used in connection with **any** program designed to assess the needs of new or continuing members. The "Interest Inventory" (Exercise

9) can be easily completed during a regular meeting, then used by the officers to help them plan future programs that will appeal to the membership.

Whether you choose whole-group methods, the pledge approach or the Big/Little Brother/Sister Program (or a combination of all three) as a means of making new members feel more at home in your group, we believe:

- The enculturation process is vital to the continuing vigor, if not the survival, of your group.
- The new member who persists as a member without having been trained in the culture of the group (either formally or informally) is **extremely** rare.

Learning to Say Good-bye Graciously

What about those members who decide to leave the group?

The educational techniques we have mentioned in this chapter have as their purpose to enlighten new members about the people, programs, policies and parameters of the group. There is always the possibility that some new members, no matter **how** welcome they are made to feel, will simply not be comfortable. Allow them to make a graceful exit. It will do no good (and perhaps will cause a great deal of harm) to try to keep a member who does not believe in what most of the group believes in. And smile as you say good-bye . . . that person is now free to explore other groups that hold the promise of meeting his or her needs . . . your group hasn't falied, there simply wasn't a match.

It's also possible to lose a few continuing members during the course of a year, even some who have been the organization's pride and joy . . . the perfect members. Unfortunately, many organizations tend to be selfish in situations like this. There is a natural feeling of "you can't leave now—how will we function in the future?—We need you!" Officers wring their hands and feel that the organization is failing, that it's not meeting the needs of the members. If the migration is massive, this could be true. Still, "crises" like this can be healthy for groups, **if** they bring about real introspection on the part of the membership. (See Chapter 10, Evaluation.)

What is often overlooked when long-time members leave the group is that possibly their personal priorities have changed and the exit of these members is simply an admission to the entire group of their changing needs. The least an organization can do with a situation like this is to simply bid them farewell, thank them for their interest, and remember them as cherished members of the organization. Too often, though, the members that remain tend to give ex-members dishonorable discharges. This is one of the most damaging things an organization can do; it does nothing but leave a bitter taste in the mouths of **all** concerned. Recognize them for their contributions to the organization, for you may find out that many benefits will accrue to your organization as these former members take on new roles as alumni.

EIGHT PRACTICAL GETTING-ACQUAINTED EXERCISES

In this chapter, we have presented examples of and prescriptions for dealing with first impressions and stereotypes, factors that affect all organizations regardless of their size, reputation or activities. Only those organizations that are empathetic and sensitive to the effects of first impressions and stereotypes can face them squarely and emerge intact and ready to do business.

The eight practical getting-acquainted exercises that follow will enable you to achieve this goal. They can be used with new members, continuing members, or officers at regular meetings or weekend retreats. People who know each others' interests, likes, skills, and sensitivities will make a happier, more productive team. It **is** worth the time it takes.

EXERCISE 2

"WHO AM I?: A GETTING-ACQUAINTED ACTIVITY"[1]

(45 minutes)

Goal: To allow participants to become acquainted quickly in a relatively non-threatening way.

Group Size: Unlimited.

Materials:
- For each participant: one 8½" x 11" sheet of paper with the question "Who am I?" written in one-inch letters at the top.
- Pencil for each participant.
- Piece of masking tape, a safety pin or a straight pin for each participant.

Setting: Large room in which participants may move about freely.

Process:
1. Participants receive the materials and are allowed ten minutes in which to write ten different answers to the question, "Who am I?" The facilitator should stress legibility, because participants must be able to read these answers easily from a distance.
2. Each participant fastens his completed sheet to the front of his clothing.
3. Participants circulate in a cocktail-party fashion, but *without* speaking. They are instructed to make eye contact with each person they encounter.
4. The facilitator asks participants to move on to another person about every two minutes.
5. After this nonverbal phase, participants are told to return to two or three different people they thought would be interesting (or different, or of similar interests, etc.). They may now talk with each other. They may be encouraged to ask questions which they ordinarily would not.

---

1. Pfeiffer, J. William, and Jones, John E. (Eds.), *A Handbook of Structured Experiences for Human Relations Training,* Volume I (Rev.). La Jolla, CA: University Associates, 1974, pp. 19-29. Used with permission.

Variations:

- Instead of the question "Who am I?," participants can be instructed to complete the open-ended statement, "I am becoming the kind of person who . . . " Another focus can be made by using the incomplete sentence, "I am pretending that..." (It is important that at least ten different responses be called for, so that participants move beyond superficial self-disclosure.)
- Participants may be asked to avoid giving demographic data in their answers. The facilitator may illustrate by pointing out the difference between "What am I?" (husband, father, counselor, etc.) and "Who am I?" (a taker of risks, managing myself toward openness, a tense person, etc.).
- Self-descriptive adjectives can be called for instead of answers to the question. A second column of adjectives could be in response to the question, "How would I like to be?"
- Participants may be permitted to speak in Process 3.
- After the processing, participants can tape their sheets to a wall, so that the complete getting-acquainted data are available for study at all times. Persons may be encouraged to edit their sheets at any time during the training event.
- As a closure activity, participants may be instructed to write what they learned during the training. The type of learning or topic may vary. For example, in a personal growth laboratory the topic can be, "What I learned about me"; in a leadership-management development laboratory, the topic could simply be, "What I learned" or "What I am going to do differently."

EXERCISE 3

"WHO AM I?" VARIATIONS:
A GETTING-ACQUAINTED ACTIVITY[2]

(45 minutes)

Goal: To allow participants to become acquainted quickly in a relatively stress-free way. (These variations may be especially appropriate for participants who have difficulty writing about themselves, as in "Who Am I?.")

---

2. Pfeiffer, J. William, and Jones, John E. (Eds.), *A Handbook of Structured Experiences for Human Relations Training,* Volume III (Rev.). La Jolla, CA: University Associates, 1974, pp. 3-5. Used with permission.

Group Size: Unlimited.

Materials:
- Sheets of paper, 12" x 20", one to be fastened around each participant's neck "bib-style," with a string.
- Ball of string and scissors.
- Pencils or felt-tipped markers.

Setting: Large room in which participants may move freely.

Process:
1. Participants receive the materials and are allowed ten minutes for any of the following activities to introduce themselves to fellow participants. The facilitator may choose one variation for all participants or allow participants to choose any variation they wish.
   a. Participants may draw a picture or pictures of themselves: a caricature, a cartoon strip, etc.
   b. Participants may draw a pie with different-sized wedges to illustrate percentages of themselves devoted to certain life focuses—for example, a love-distribution pie or an energy pie.
   c. Participants may draw a "lifeline"—a graph of their lives to the present, showing high points—or a projected total lifeline which indicates where they are now or where they want to go.
   d. Participants may write a series of words, such as adjectives. Words might be selected through free association.
   e. Specialty groups, such as musicians, engineers or chemists, may identify themselves with their own symbols.
   f. Participants may draw pictures of animals, objects or music with which they identify.
   g. Participants may write words to indicate their own values.
2. Each participant ties his completed sheet around his neck.
3. Participants circulate in cocktail-party fashion, but *without* speaking. (Background music is optional.)
4. The facilitator asks participants to move on to a new person every minute for a total of ten to fifteen "meetings."
5. After this nonverbal phase, the participants are told to return to two or three people they think would be interesting, different, etc., based on their previous encounters. They may now speak to one another. They may be encouraged to ask questions they ordinarily would not ask.

Variations: This exercise lends itself to the same variations as Exercise 2.

EXERCISE 4

PERSON-TO-PERSON NAME TAGS: SHARING QUESTIONS AND ANSWERS

(45 minutes - 1 hour)

How to Use This Exercise: This is an adaption we've made of "Who Am I?" that can be used effectively when groups get together for the first time (or early in their association). Depending upon your needs, the questions can be changed to elicit more meaningful responses from the members. This exercise can be used simply as a means of helping new members get to know each other in a very relaxing way or can be tailored to bring fairly "heavy" group concerns out into the open.

Group Size: 20 on up.

Materials:
- One 8½" x 11" sheet of sturdy paper or cardboard for each participant with string tied through each of the upper corners so that it can be hung around the neck at chest height. (We've found that manila folders cut in half work very well.)
- A pencil or small marker for each participant.
- A chalkboard.

Setting: Any meeting room cleared of furniture so that participants can circulate freely.

Process:
1. The facilitator asks that members form pairs, stressing that the experience will be more meaningful if the two persons don't already know each other. Ask that they designate one person as participant A and the other as participant B.
2. The facilitator then writes the following items on the chalkboard, and instructs the participants to write them on their nametags, leaving enough space between each for written responses.
   a. Name
   b. What were your reasons for attending the meeting tonight (today)?
   c. How do you most like to spend your leisure time?
   d. What one thing really "turns you off?"
   e. What is your Zodiac sign?

3. The participants exchange nametags, and participant A proceeds to "interview" participant B about B's answers to each of the items. As B explains the responses, A writes them in the appropriate place on B's nametag (stress legibility!).
4. The process is repeated, with B asking the questions and recording A's responses.
5. Once both nametags have been completed (allow about 10 minutes for each), ask the participants to put their own nametags on and then request that they circulate without talking, reading each others responses. They should spend no more than two minutes with each person.
6. After each person has had between 5-8 encounters, instruct the participants to seek out two or three people they would like to get to know better based on what they read on the nametags. Allow about 15 minutes for verbal exchange.

EXERCISE 5

INTERVIEWS AND INTRODUCTIONS

(20 minutes plus one minute for each group member)

How to Use This Exercise: This is a good way to begin a meeting when the majority of the people in the group are newcomers.

Group Size: 10-40 (because of time/attention span limitations)

Materials:
• Paper and pencil for each participant.

Setting: Any meeting room.

Process:
1. Ask each member to pair off with another member and to designate themselves as participants A and B.
2. Have A interview B for ten minutes asking whatever questions he feels are appropriate.
3. Repeat the process, with B asking questions of A.
4. Allow a few minutes for group members to organize their thoughts/notes.

5. Have each member introduce his/her partner to the whole group. If necessary, signal the speaker at the end of one minute.
6. The exercise may be ended with the last introduction, or the facilitator may ask the group to discuss their reactions to the experience. If the response is slow, guide the group by asking specific questions:
   a. How do you feel about the group now?
   b. How did you feel when you first came in?
   c. Which person in the group do you feel closest to? Why?
   d. What has happened here?

EXERCISE 6

LISTENING AND INFERRING: A GETTING-ACQUAINTED ACTIVITY[3]

(15 minutes)

Goal: To facilitate the involvement of individuals in a newly-formed group.

Group Size: Unlimited.

Setting: Meeting room large enough to disperse participants and reduce noise interference.

Process:
1. Form groups of three. The criterion for formation is not knowing the other members of the triad.
2. Participants in each group name themselves A, B or C.
   a. Participant A takes three minutes to tell the other two persons as much about himself as he feels comfortable in doing. Then B and C take two minutes to tell A what they heard him say. They also tell him what they infer (or assume) from what he said or left unsaid.
   b. The process is repeated, with participant B telling about himself. A and C then tell what they heard and inferred.
   c. In the final round, participant C tells about himself, and A and B repeat what they heard and tell their inferences.

---

3. Pfeiffer, J. William, and Jones, John E. (Eds.) *A Handbook of Structured Experiences for Human Relations Training,* Volume I (Rev.). La Jolla, CA: University Associates, 1974, pp. 3-4. Used with permission.

Variations:
- All three participants can tell about themselves before the others respond.
- After each participant tells about himself, the communication becomes two-way in order for the listeners to check on the accuracy of their listening and inferring.
- The two listeners can be assigned different tasks. One listens to make a paraphrase, and the other listens to draw inferences.
- The content can be changed from getting acquainted to exploring points of view about an issue that is relevant to the group.

EXERCISE 7

FIRST NAMES, FIRST IMPRESSIONS:
A FEEDBACK EXPERIENCE [4]

(Approximately 1 hour)

Goals:
- To get acquainted with other members of a small group.
- To discover one's initial impact on others.
- To study phenomena related to first impressions—their accuracy and effects.

Group Size: Six to 12 participants.

Materials:
- Two sheets of paper and a pencil for each participant.

Setting: Group members should be seated in a circle, with lapboards for writing.

---

4. Pfeiffer, J. William, and Jones, John E. (Eds.) *A Handbook of Structured Experiences for Human Relations Training*, Volume II (Rev.). La Jolla, CA: University Associates, 1974, pp. 88-89. Used with permission.

Process:

1. At the first meeting of the group, the facilitator directs that each person give his first name and one or two significant facts about himself.
2. Participants are then instructed to turn their chairs around, away from the circle, so that they cannot see the other group members. They are told to write down as many of the first names as they can remember.
3. After about three minutes, they turn their chairs back toward the group and find out whose names they forgot. They may ask for additional information to attach to the names that they found difficult to remember.
4. The group discusses names, feelings attached to them, difficulties experienced in remembering them, and reactions of those whose names were not remembered.
5. The facilitator hands out additional sheets of paper, and participants are directed to write a group roster (names in the same order on each). Then they are asked to note briefly their first impressions of each group member.
6. These first-impressions papers are collected by the facilitator. Without revealing the identity of the writers, he reads all impressions of the first participant, who is then asked to comment on the accuracy of the impressions, his feelings while hearing them, and surprising items. Then all impressions of the second participant are read aloud, he reacts, and so on.
7. The group members discuss the accuracy of first-impression data, the effects of first impressions, and their reactions to this experience.

Variations:

- Each participant reads aloud his first impressions of each of the other members of the group.
- *Present* impressions can be substituted for first impressions, if participants have known each other before.
- *First and present* impressions can be used.
- Participants can be instructed to predict what impressions they will hear.
- Participants can be encouraged to include *negative* and *puzzling* impressions of each other.
- The person receiving feedback can be directed to make a poster displaying what everyone says about him.

EXERCISE 8

"LITTLEST ANGEL BOXES"

(15 minutes to 1 hour)

How to Use This Exercise: We have found this exercise to be useful in two different situations:
1. As a means of introducing group officers to the membership at meetings held early in the year.
2. As a means of "opening up" new conversations with a group that has both old and new members in it. It is an excellent way to begin to identify members with similar interests and values.

Group Size: Six on up.

Setting: Any meeting room with moveable chairs.

Process: (When used as a means of officer introduction)
1. Bring the book *The Littlest Angel* to an executive meeting and either read or paraphrase the story so that the officers understand the concept of a "Littlest Angel Box." (In brief, the littlest angel was a small boy who died and when he went to Heaven, he was extremely unhappy because he had left a box full of his most valuable possessions under his bed on earth. He was granted permission to fetch it, and was much more content once it was in his possession. When the Christ Child was to be born, all the residents of Heaven brought wonderful and rich gifts to the throne of God, so that He could choose one to present to the Child. All the littlest angel had to give was his box—which he did—and God chose it because it contained things of the earth that a human child would love. The box began to glow, rose in the sky, and became the Star of Bethlehem.)
2. Ask the officers to bring "Littlest Angel Boxes" of their own to share with the membership—they are to contain things or representations of things that are personally valued by each person (3 - 10 items).
3. At the beginning of the meeting each officer, in turn, takes 5 - 10 minutes to explain the articles in his box, telling why the items are important to him.

Process: (When used with the entire membership.)
1. Begin by having the officers share their boxes with the membership during a meeting early in the year.
2. Announce that at the next meeting, anyone who wants to should bring a box to share with the group.
3. At the end of the next meeting, allow those who have not brought their boxes to leave, then begin the following process with those who remain.
4. If the group is larger than eight, break them into sub-groups so that there are between six and eight in each group.
5. Allow each person 5 - 10 minutes to share the contents of his / her box with the group, answering questions and explaining the reasons for the inclusion of each item, etc.
6. Allow time for people with similar items to get together and discuss them.

Note: This exercise is not limited to use by religious organizations. We have used it successfully in the classroom, and in meetings of groups with varied purposes. It is not the content of the story of The Littlest Angel that is of great importance, rather the process of identifying personal values and being willing to share those values with other people.

EXERCISE 9

THE INTEREST INVENTORY

The purpose of the interest inventory is three-fold: 1) to determine what activities will probably be popular with the newcomers to the group; 2) to aid the leadership in identifying new members with particular skills who could be of great assistance to the group; and 3) to facilitate new member self-assessment and private commitment in an atmosphere that is relatively free from threat. In the case of an outdoor recreation group, for example, an interest inventory might look something like this:

SIERRA CLUB INTEREST INVENTORY

Name_____ Phone # _____

Address _____

Do you have a car? Yes _____   No _____
If so, would you be willing to drive your car when you go on an

outing?   Yes _____   No _____

Please indicate your interests and special skills below. This
information will only be used by the group to plan this year's
activities; you will in no way be obligated to participate in any of
the activities by virtue of your responses on this inventory.

Activity	I am not at all interested	I am interested	I have had some experience	I can lead an outing	I can teach others to lead outings
Back-packing					
Snowskiing					
Skin Diving					
Day Hikes					
Mountain-eering					
Snow Camping					
River Rafting					
Spelunking (Caving)					
Rock-Climbing					
Other					

COMMENTS: _____

As is obvious, the inventory will have meaning *only* if all possible alternatives are listed. If the officers list only those that appeal to *them* the members won't really be making the choices and the information gathered will be worthless.

Once the inventory has been administered to the membership and collected, it has many valuable uses.

- It can be used to plan activities that will draw a large number of participants.
- Officers will be able to approximate the general skill level of the members and thus can avoid planning activities that will either be too advanced or not challenging enough for the majority of the group.
- It is a means of identifying new members who may need special attention/introduction.
- It serves as a resource file for officers when choosing committee chairmen for specialized tasks.
- It aids in identifying people who might be interested in/suited for future positions of leadership in the group.
- It might be used to establish special interest sub-groups within the group to work on tasks that they are particularly interested in.
- The results can be made available to the membership so that on their own, people can contact others with similar interests and abilities.

Since the interest inventory can be written, completed and compiled in a very short period of time, it is an excellent way to let members know that the leadership of the group is concerned about what "the people" want to do. It not only provides guidelines for future activities, but establishes confidence in tasks or problem-solving situations (including member need-assessment).

PART II

Introduction:

Leadership Is . . .
Flexibility and Productivity

Part II contains a great deal of information that is **essential** for good, solid leadership. Since we believe that the chapter titles are fairly self-explanatory for this section, we won't go into a summary of each one here, but we heartily encourage everyone who now holds a position of leadership as well as those who would like to be in a position of leadership to read this material thoroughly.

The basics of conducting meetings, creating interest and maintaining continuity are described in detail for review or first reading. This is the "nuts and bolts" section; the place for you to find or renew the necessary background and fundamentals you need for dynamic leadership.

Some meetings go on forever
Others seem hardly to start
The ones that I like best
Are those that have a heart.

Point of order! I object!
They're all in the little blue book
But amendments can be friendly
And so can the "Gobble-de-Gook:"

CHAPTER 4

Making Each Meeting Everybody's Business

Today's leader must be competent in presiding over business meetings where goals are set and where plans of action to achieve these goals are developed. Relating well to other officers and to the general membership will make your job a lot easier and the productivity of your organization more gratifying. The purpose of this chapter, therefore, is to give you some basic "how-to" information which will make the job of presiding officer a little more manageable.

Since meetings are where all major decisions are made by the entire membership, knowing how to plan for and conduct them will keep you from bogging down.

The First Meeting Of The Year

The first meeting of the year is a special challenge for any president or chairperson, since it "sets the mood" for all future meetings of the organization.

It also gives members, especially new ones, that important first impression of the promise the group may or may not hold for them in terms of meeting their needs or sustaining their interest.

Here are some suggestions that will help make this meeting a success.

Getting Ready

1. Make sure the meeting place can be easily identified from the outside. Place a sign outside the building and on the door of the meeting room announcing the name of the group and the fact that new members are welcome.

2. Have officers and regular members at the door to greet people and to make sure that all newcomers get a name tag.

3. Be prepared to collect dues and issue membership cards.

4. Have everyone fill out a pre-designed card so you will have a record of who attended: name, address, telephone number, interests, etc. (See Chapter 8,

"Organizational Resource Information Card"). Cards are better than a list of names on a sheet because you can get more information and the cards can be sorted for different uses.

5. Give careful thought to the seating plan of the room (See Chapter 5, "Traditional Seating Design") and be sure that there are enough chairs for everyone.

6. If the meeting is being held in a large auditorium, check out the public address system **early**, not just before you want to use it.

7. Start on time . . . at the first meeting and at every meeting. Members soon learn from experience whether you are an "on-the-dot" starter or a chair who starts 15 or 20 minutes late. Further, not starting on time when people have come on time is a way of telling them that **their** time is less important than that of the people you are waiting for. Don't do it.

Introductions

1. Introduce yourself. "Hi, everybody. My name is Charlie Brown, and I'll be serving as your president during the coming year. I work at the supermarket down the street and go to school part-time at the community college. My wife, Susan, and our two children are here today, and I'd like you to meet them, too."

2. Welcome all new people attending, giving them individual recognition if at all possible. Let them briefly introduce themselves if time allows. "It's good to see so many new members here today, would all the people who are here for the first time please stand? Thanks. Would each of you tell us a little about yourself so we can become better acquainted?" (For large membership, this best done in small buzz groups and other methods described in Chapter 5.)

3. Welcome all returning members, and give them individual recognition similar to that afforded newcomers.

4. Acknowledge members who have achieved special recognition (e.g.: community leaders, scholarship recipients, class or school officers, etc.).

5. Have each officer participate in the meeting in some major way.

Objectives, History & Traditions

1. Explain the purpose of the group. You might want to distribute a copy of the constitution and bylaws or a brochure about the organization's purpose, history and traditions.

2. Explain the formal organizational structure of the group (using visual aids for this will be a big help).

3. Review the major past accomplishments of your organization. Display photographs, trophies, scrapbooks, etc., when appropriate.

4. Review recent activities and continuing projects of the group that will require effort on the part of the membership in the future.

Outlining Plans for the Year

1. Announce important dates and events that will guide the group's activities. Distribute a tentative calendar of upcoming events during the first meeting. Allow time for new members to ask questions or make suggestions.

2. Explain important decisions the group may face during the year.

3. Announce standing committee appointments or name the appointments that need to be made and tell members how they can get on a committee.

4. Encourage the membership to suggest program ideas such as speakers, films, etc. Some groups give each member a card on which to jot down ideas and collect them at the end of the first meeting.

Just for Fun

1. Have an auction, a drawing, a simple contest, or play a silly game. "Before we have refreshments, let's form a big circle in the middle of the room. Your position in the circle will be determined by the first letter in your first name . . . alphabetically, with the "A's" up here in this corner and the "Z's" over there."
2. Have old members demonstrate a hobby or share a special interest.
3. Show slides or movies of past activities of the group.
4. Invite a good speaker.
5. Have refreshments.

Ending the Meeting

1. Announce the next meeting—date, time, place, main items of business and program.
2. End the meeting at a high point of interest, not when members are exhausted and impatient to leave.

Standard Business Meetings

All organizations have business meetings, some formal—like the City Council or Board of Trustees—others less formal like the Women's Garden Club or a parents' organization. One thing is absolute, however, **a business meeting is everybody's business, every** member's. It's not just the concern of the presiding officer and the executive committee; it's not just the "private forum" for the members who have the courage to speak out. The wise president sees to it that everyone knows what is going on and has a positive opportunity to participate. Use the following sections only as a guide and change it to fit your needs as appropriate.

Involving Everybody

Everybody should:

1. Be invited to attend and be informed about the meeting

date, time and place. Put a sign on the door to let them know they've found the right room. And how about a "Welcome . . . come in"?

2. Know in advance what important decisions are to be made.

3. See the agenda before the meeting starts or at least have access to it when they walk into the meeting room; they should also have the opportunity to question any item or to add an item before the "agenda is closed."

4. Be able to see and hear what's going on.

5. Understand the meaning of every proposed action and what their options are.

6. Have all the facts, alternatives and consequences, and the opportunity to discuss informally every major issue before voting. (See Chapter 5, "Making Your Discussions Informal.")

7. Participate in the selection of individuals to chair and serve on committees.

8. Have access to all information available to any other member or officer.

Preparing the Agenda

The agenda comes from a review of correspondence, from past minutes, and from committee assignments and goals, and it includes consideration of future events on the calendar. Check with people who are due to give reports to be sure they are ready; do this before you place them on the agenda or **at least** before you call on them. (Meetings lose momentum in a hurry when cluttered with several "no reports" or shoddy reporting.) Some organizations review the agenda in executive committee sessions just before the meeting to make sure it is complete and everybody is ready. These sessions are also useful in spreading the work of the meeting around and in getting maximum involvement of the officers. The officers should all get to the meeting **early** to visit with members as they arrive and to help get the meeting room completely set up and checked out. Agendas can be as simple or as complex as the organization requires to carry on its business. For the Cub Scouts, for example, it can be as simple as this:

CUB SCOUT PACK 12 MEETING AGENDA

Friday Evening, October 10
Emerson School . . . Room 103
7:00   Dens meet and take roll
7:15   Pack meeting begins. (Mr. Mulder)
      (1) Introductions
      (2) Reports
      (3) Announcements
7:30   Boy Scout Troop 5, First Aid
      Demonstration (Mr. Chandler)
7:45   Awards (Mrs. Beck & Mr. Gersten)
8:00   Refreshments (Mrs. Spry & Mr. Walters)

Next meeting: Friday, November 12

For a more formal organization, the agenda should be informational and thought-provoking, not just a list of topics. On the next two pages is an example of such an agenda; it should be mailed to the members in advance and also made available to everyone at the door!

PANACEA UNIVERSITY

Academic Senate Agenda

Meeting No. 16, May 10, 1978, 3:10 p.m.
Faculty Office Building, Room 202

1. **Quorum Count:** 44 voting members; 23 required present.

2. **Minutes approval:** Meeting #15 (distributed 4/15/78).

3. **Agenda approval:** (distributed 5/8/78).

4. **Introduction of Guests:**
   a. Dr. Mary B. Alexander, Academic Vice President
   b. Others (if any)

5. **Officer Reports:** (none)

6. **Committee Reports:**
   a. Personnel Policies (Dr. Jorgensen)
      (1) Progress report on accessibility to personal records
      (2) Proposed resolution on faculty evaluation by students
   b. Library (Dr. Hurtado)
      (1) Proposal to increase Xerox copy services to faculty

7. **Business Items:**

   a. Possible adoption of amendment to statements on professional ethics: (See meeting #14, page 3.)

   b. Possible approval of refurbishing plan and $15,496.00 allocation for faculty lounge. (See meeting #13, attachment B.)

8. **Discussion Items:**

   a. Proposed policy on room names in academic areas (Dr. Howard)

   b. Status of plan to combine psychology and education departments (Dr. Sorenson)

9. **Announcements:**

   a. Deadline for sabbatical leave requests is June 3.

   b. There is an opening on the curriculum coordinating committee from the School of Engineering. Contact Dr. Chandler, ext. 2491.

   c. Next meeting: June 11 at 3:10 p.m.

   d. Others, if any (from the membership)

   _____

   _____

   _____

There may be variations to the above order, of course.
General letters are usually read by the secretary after the reading of minutes and specific letters just prior to the discussion of that matter on the agenda. Some organizations take up staff reports after officer reports, many make a distinction between standing committees and special committees. Business items are sometimes called "old business," and discussion items are often combined with reports.

Presiding and Other Things

The presiding officer of a business meeting has five major responsibilities:[1]

1. **The responsibility to initiate** items or proposals for the members to consider; to bring before the group matters on which they may want to take action.

Here are some suggestions about how to get a discussion initiated:

a. A committee report generally provides a statement of the problem and either a recommended solution or a number of alternative solutions. (See Chapter 6, "Selecting and Instructing Committees.") In a formal setting, the discussion follows a motion and its second, e.g., "I move to accept the recommendation," or "I move to accept alternative number three."

b. An officer or another member can make a brief explanation of a problem or an item that needs group action and can make a motion, e.g., "I move that we change our meeting time to Wednesdays at 7 p.m."

c. The presiding officer can explain a situation that needs attention and request a motion so that it can be discussed.

d. Any member can initiate a discussion by making a motion and having it seconded by another member. "I move that Chi Chapter of the Alpha Gamma Rho Fraternity donate $100 for the improvement of parking at Cuesta Park."

2. **The responsibility to facilitate** the deliberations and actions of the group in order to make it easier for them to conduct the business which has brought them together.

The key facilitation is making a two-hour meeting seem like 60 minutes. It **can** be done if you . . .

---

1. From Sutherland, Sidney S., *When You Preside.* Danville, Ill.: The Interstate Printers & Publishers, Inc., 1969, pp. 101-108. Used with permission.

a. **Know your parliamentary procedure**. (See the chart at the end of this chapter.)

b. Use a parliamentarian. (See "Using a Parliamentarian" later in this chapter.)

c. **Keep things moving**. Avoid making long explanations or speeches. Your job isn't to give facts, it's to initiate and coordinate. If you **do** have information to give, wait until all others have spoken; others have facts too . . . let them contribute.

d. **Turn over the chair**. If you feel you **must** speak about an issue, don't do it as presiding officer; ask the Vice President to serve until the motion has been disposed of. "Call on" people to make reports; don't "turn over the chair" to them.

e. **Use your secretary**. Don't try to remember the exact wording of motions. Ask the secretary to repeat them as they are made to be certain they are clear and the wording is correct before accepting it for the second and discussion.

f. **Keep your eyes open**. Watch the members all the time to catch their non-verbal cues indicating their readiness to speak, their agreement or disagreement. It will help you give recognition and to keep things moving.

g. **Use your authority**. No one can speak without recognition from you; you carry considerable responsibility in determining when to bring a motion to a vote and you decide and state whether a motion has passed or has been defeated. Don't hesitate to use your gavel if you want to keep things moving.

h. **Handle business by general consent where appropriate**. If the matter under discussion obviously has the unanimous approval of all the membership, don't go through the process of asking for a motion, etc. Bring the matter to a close. "It seems that we are in general agreement that we do such and such, are there any objections? Hearing none, it is so ordered."

3. **The responsibility to orient** and guide the group in the conduct of its business.

Parliamentary procedure has a language of its own, and if even a portion of your membership doesn't speak it or understand it, your role as interpreter becomes critical if you want everyone to know what's going on and what their options are at any point in the parliamentary process. Assuming you know parliamentary procedure, it it your responsibility as president to help the "un-initiated" through the process.

At the very elementary level, when a main motion is seconded and is on the floor for discussion, you may say, "This motion can be discussed, amended, referred to a committee, or perhaps you are ready to vote on it. What is your pleasure?" Tell them if the required vote must be a simple majority or a two-thirds majority.

The goal is to orient members to the parliamentary situation, guide them through each step, interpret the meaning of motions, tell them their options, and do all this without putting anyone down or intimidating anyone with your parliamentary wisdom.

4. **The responsibility to encourage** and bring about a free and complete discussion of matters brought before the meeting; to act as a mediator when debate gets a little aggressive.

Members often get the floor and immediately start a discussion. Don't permit this or the meeting will tend to become a series of miscellaneous discussions, longer and longer, without much real business being transacted. Be ready with the question, "Do you wish to state that in the form of a motion, Margie?" or "Will you please put that in the form of a motion?" Then ask for a second, and the matter is ready to be discussed.

In managing the discussion of a motion, there are a few simple guidelines:

a. Make every effort to keep the discussion balanced, alternating speakers for and against the motion.

b. Try to give every member a chance to speak once on

a motion before any member is permitted to speak twice.

c. Keep speakers on the subject when their comments have wandered . . . "Thank you, Fred. Now the question we are discussing is 'Shall we donate $100 for the improvement of parking facilities at Cuesta Park? Is there any further discussion on the question?''

d. When the group is too large for everyone to have a chance to speak, or if some of the members are too shy to speak out because of the size of the audience, divide the membership into small buzz groups. (See Chapter 5, "Using Buzz Groups.")

e. Write the motion under discussion on a chalkboard or overhead projector to keep the membership continuously aware of the question. This will reduce extraneous comments and shorten the meeting.

f. If the subject is rather complex and more facts are needed to reach a high quality decision, suggest a motion to postpone, or a motion to refer the matter to a committee:

> "It appears that this matter requires considerably more thought and discussion than we can give it tonight; would someone like to move that we postpone this question to the next meeting?"

Or:

> "It seems that we need more information on this matter before going further; do I hear a motion to refer this question to a committee?"

5. **The responsibility to summarize**, clarify and restate motions made and considered by the group prior to voting.

Summarizing the key points made during the discussion helps to reduce redundancy and suggests readiness to take action, either by consensus or by voting. If there is no general agreement, after summarizing, ask, "Are you ready for the question?" Then, if there is no objection, put it to a vote.

Knowing What to Do With a Motion

Some things you should know about motions:

1. **A motion should be made and seconded** before **any** discussion starts.

2. **You should state the motion** after it has been made and seconded and then ask for any discussion.

3. **The maker of the motion** has a right to be the first to discuss it.

4. **Only one main motion** may be considered at a time.

5. **If a motion to amend is made and seconded**, the proposed amendment must be voted upon **before** a vote is taken on the main motion to which it applies.

6. **A main motion may be changed** without being formally amended by another motion. This may be done by the maker of the main motion accepting the change as a "friendly amendment."

7. **When a member says "question"**, it means "I am ready for the question or ready to vote". When a member says, "I call for the question" or "I move the previous question," a motion is being made to stop debate and to vote immediately.

8. **To bring a motion to vote** say, "Are you ready for the question?" (Members are saying "yes" when they respond with "question!") "The question has been called. All those in favor say 'Aye'; all those opposed say 'Nay'. The motion is carried (or defeated)." If some members appear not to vote, you may ask, "Does anyone abstain?" (Rap the gavel whenever a group decision has been reached.)

9. **All votes take a simple majority except** those that somehow inhibit the right of members to speak; these motions require a two-thirds vote.

* vote immediately
* limit debate or extend the limits to debate
* object to considering a question
* close nominations
* postpone to a definite time by a special order
* suspend the rules

10. **Whenever a vote requiring a two-thirds majority** is taken, ask for a hand vote or a standing vote. This will save time since invariably someone will call "division" which demands a visual vote and you will have to call for the vote again. (It's impossible to **hear** two-thirds anyway!)

A **"majority vote"** is one more than half of those voting.

A **"two-thirds vote"** is two-thirds of the votes cast. (Do not count abstentions.)

A **"plurality"** involves three or more choices and means more votes than any other candidate or alternative. (A plurality does not decide the issue unless there is a special or standing rule to that effect.)

11. **The chairperson may vote** on every issue or may choose to vote only to swing the outcome one way or the other.

12. **Motions are ranked** and placed in categories: (See the chart at the end of this chapter for a complete table of motions.)

a. **A main motion** is one that brings an item of business before the group for action. It has the lowest rank which means that any of the rest can legally be made when a main motion is on the floor.

b. **A subsidiary motion** is one to amend, postpone, limit debate or refer the main motion. These are second lowest in rank and only take precedence over a main motion.

c. **An incidental motion** pertains to the method of conducting business: point of order, parliamentary inquiry, division of the assembly and withdrawing a motion. They take precedence over both the main motions and subsidiary motions.

d. **A privileged motion** involves an immediate action of the group as a whole: that they recess or adjourn. It ranks over all other motions and can be made whenever any other motion is being considered.

13. **A "Quorum"** is the number of members eligible to vote that are required to be present in order to transact

business legally. Their number is generally stated in the bylaws of the organization.

Strictly correct parliamentary procedure is more complex than this review of some of the most common practices. The chart included at the end of this chapter graphically shows the "Principal Rules Governing Motions"; but for a thorough presentation of the how and why of modern parliamentary practice we recommend **Learning Parliamentary Procedure**, or **Sturgis Standard Code of Parliamentary Procedure**, both by Alice Sturgis. (Alice Sturgis is described in a feature article in the **San Francisco Chronicle** February 25, 1973 as "the woman who made Roberts Rules of Order obsolete.")

Using a Parliamentarian

Even if you think you know parliamentary procedures quite well, have an **expert** handy when the details start piling up in a heated business meeting. Remember the parliamentarian is your personal assistant, and the conversation between you should be fairly private. Only when you cannot explain the parliamentary situation to the membership should you ever ask for a public explanation from your parliamentary assistant.

Writing the Minutes

One of the most important administrative tasks of an organization is that of keeping the official records of the group's business: the writing of concise, readable and accurate minutes of each meeting. During the meeting, the secretary is just about as active as the president. In fact, the secretary is so involved with keeping track of what's going on that it's seldom possible to get involved in discussions, even though the secretary is a regular member of the organization. The secretary works along with the president and helps by following the agenda and taking complete notes. Although generally not an authority on parliamentary procedure, the secretary will benefit from knowing the basic principles so that the minutes are absolutely correct on this point.

Note Taking: Taking complete, accurate notes during the meeting is essential to being able to write good minutes of the meeting later, and it involves:

a. Being ready with all correspondence received since the last meeting that may have to be read.
b. Reading correspondence as directed by the president.
c. Reading the minutes of the previous meeting as directed by the president.
d. Listening to the content of a motion and reading aloud what you understand it to be; plus getting feedback from the maker of the motion to be absolutely certain that it is correct before the president asks for a second. (This should also be done when motions are made in writing and given to the secretary.)
e. Recording the name of the maker of the motion and the name of the seconder.
f. Letting the president know when a motion does not have a second before discussion.
g. Being ready to respond to the president's, "Will you please read the question?" ("The question" is always the exact wording of the motion on the floor.)
h. Recording the exact vote on all matters that require a two-thirds majority and those that are taken when a "division" or "roll call" is requested.
i. Having the membership list ready to check the quorum before the meeting is called to order and to handle a roll-call vote whenever one is requested by a member.

j. Getting the signatures of all those present (if sign-in attendance is a standing rule or tradition of the organization).

k. Getting copies of all reports presented at the meeting, along with the name(s) of those who participated in the presentation.

l. Getting the names of all guests who make presentations. (It is sometimes important to get titles and affiliations, too.)

m. Recording the action taken by the group after each report or presentation.

n. Keeping track of time limitations on individuals or agenda items unless the president assigns someone else to do it.

o. Getting the names (sometimes the addresses, telephone numbers, and times available for meetings) of people who have agreed to carry out a task or to work on a committee.

The Minutes: Why? It is well to understand the purposes served by the final and official minutes of a business meeting before getting into how to write them.

a. They are the official and legal record of the organization.

b. They inform members who could not attend about what happened.

c. They help in following up on assignments and decisions.

d. They help in formulating the agenda for the next meeting.

e. They give continuity to the procedures, traditional activities, etc., of the organization.

f. They are a valuable review of the activities of the past and aid in report writing and formulating future activities and programs.

g. They are a valuable resource in selecting members for honors, awards, nominations, etc.

The Minutes—Telling What Happened: The method of writing the official minutes varies somewhat with the nature of the organization but these are generally accepted guidelines:

a. Name of group, type of meeting (general, regular, special continued, etc.) and place, date and time of meeting.

b. The style and format of minutes should indicate major agenda items underlined or otherwise easily identified along the left margin. (Number the pages consecutively throughout the year.)

c. Names of the persons present. (There are many variations on this point, including voting members, non-voting members, guests, absences, excused absence, proxies, tardies, etc.)

d. Quorum count, call to order and the name of the presiding officer.

e. Correction and approval of the minutes of the previous meeting (for substantive corrections, this should include the name of the person who made the request).

f. The exact wording of motions, name (no nicknames, please!) of the maker, the name of the seconder and whether the motion was passed or defeated. The exact vote is taken by "division" or "roll call." (Any member has the right to have the vote recorded in the minutes, upon request.) Sometimes "MSP" is shown to indicate "moved, seconded, and passed," and "MSF" to indicate "moved, seconded, and failed." Example:

   MSP Mary Smith/John Jones "that $100 be allocated for officer travel this year."

g. The exact wording and outcome of all subsidiary motions; e.g.: to amend, refer; etc. Example:

   MSF Bill White/Sandy Green "to amend the main motion by striking the word 'travel' and inserting the word 'expenses'." (If "division" had been called, you would record this as MSF 12-15,

PRINCIPAL RULES GOVERNING MOTIONS

Order of precedence	Can interrupt speaker?	Requires a second?	Debatable?	Amendable?
I. PRIVILEGED MOTIONS				
1. Adjourn	no	yes	no	no
2. Recess	no	yes	no	no •
3. Question of Privilege	yes	no	no	no
II. SUBSIDIARY MOTIONS				
4. Postpone Temporarily (Lay on the table)	no	yes	no	no
5. Vote Immediately (Previous question)	no	yes	no	no
6. Limit Debate	no	yes	no	yes •
7. Postpone Definitely	no	yes	yes •	yes •
8. Refer to Committee	no	yes	yes •	yes •
9. Amend	no	yes	yes	yes
10. Postpone Indefinitely	no	yes	yes	no
III. MAIN MOTIONS				
11. (a) A General Main Motion	no	yes	yes	yes
(b) Specific Main Motions				
Reconsider	yes	yes	yes	no
Rescind	no	yes	yes	no
Resume Consideration	no	yes	no	no
Create Orders	no	yes	yes •	yes •
V. INCIDENTAL MOTIONS*				
Appeal	yes	yes	yes	no
Point of Order	yes	no	no	no
Parliamentary Inquiry	yes	no	no	no
Withdraw a Motion	no	no	no	no
Suspend Rules	no	yes	no	no
Object to Consideration	yes	no	no	no
Division of a Question	no	no	no	no
Division of Assembly	yes	no	no	no

* No order of precedence among themselves. Each motion decided immediately.

2. From *Learning Parliamentary Procedure* by Alice F. Sturgis. Copyright 1953 by McGraw-Hill, Inc. Used by permission of McGraw-Hill Book Company.

Vote required?	Applies to what motions?	Motions can have what applied to it (in addition to withdraw)?	Can be renewed?
majority	no other motion	no other motion	yes •
majority	no other motion	amend•	yes •
no vote	no other motion	no other motion	no
majority	main, amend, appeal	no other motion	yes •
two-thirds	debatable motions	no other motion	yes •
two-thirds	debatable motions	amend•	yes•
majority	main motion	amend,• vote immediately, limit debate	yes•
majority	main, amend	vote immediately, limit debate	yes•
majority	variable in form	subsidiary motions, reconsider	no
majority	main motion	vote immediately, limit debate	no
majority	no motion	specific main, subsidiary, object to consideration	no
majority	main, amend, appeal	vote immediately, limit debate, postpone definitely	no
majority	main motion	all subsidiary motions	no
majority	main, amend, appeal	no other motion	yes•
majority	main motion	amend	yes•
tie or majority	decisions of chair	limit debate, vote immediately, postpone temporarily or definitely	no
no vote	any error	no other motion	no
no vote	no motion	no other motion	no
no vote	all motions	none	yes•
two-thirds	no motion	no other motion	yes•
two-thirds negative	main motion	no other motion	no
no vote	main, amend	no other motion	no
no vote	voice votes	no other motion	no

• Restricted.   • After change in parliamentary situation.

indicating that 12 "ayes" and 15 "nay" votes resulted from a hand vote.)

h. Motions such as **points of order, parliamentary inquiry** and **questions of privilege** are **not** shown in the official minutes unless they result in an action directly affecting the business transacted.

i. Main points made in debate are generally included in committee minutes (it helps them write their report or make their recommendation), but **not** generally included in the minutes of an organization's business meeting.

j. The exact wording of a committee assignment including any power to act, the date due and the names of the committee chairman and members.

k. Be brief. Be specific. Be accurate.

l. Conclude your work of art with:

"Respectfully Submitted,"

(signature)
Bobbie Brown, Secretary

When It's All Over

Leaders who are responsible for planning meetings are generally concerned about how it all turned out. The most valid evaluation of how it went is appropriately placed in the hands of the members as well as the officers. (See Chapter 10, "Meeting Evaluation Form" for a sample questionnaire which can be completed in a few minutes at the end of the meeting.) Officers should review this feedback before the next meeting and make the required changes.

If this explanation of how to conduct a standard business meeting seems too stiff or formal for your organization, be sure to read the next chapter. In it we'll discuss how you can give variety and flexibility to regular meetings of your group.

Large meetings are bummers
As everyone knows
Especially when set up
In columns and rows.

So why not form circles
Of six or of eight?
This is the setting
In which to create.

CHAPTER 5

Variety is the Spice of Meetings

It was a perceptive person who first coined the phrase: "Variety is the spice of life." We all want variety in our work and in our play; wouldn't it be refreshing if we could have a little variety in our meetings too?

A by-the-book standard business meeting may satisfy the appetite or expectancies of the board of directors of a large corporation, but then, maybe no one ever asked them how they feel about spice. For members of volunteer groups, however, variety at meetings and activities just might be the important ingredient that keeps people coming back for more.

Making Your Discussions Informal

"I move that we discuss this matter informally," said Diana.

"I second the motion," said Sidney.

"It has been moved and seconded to discuss this matter informally."

"Is there any discussion on this motion?"

"Seeing none, we shall vote."

"All in favor please say 'Aye'."

"All those opposed please say 'Nay'."

At this point a member abstaining may interject, "I abstain!"

"The motion is carried, and we shall discuss this matter informally."

That's all it takes at a formal business meeting to open it up to any of the upcoming informal procedures. But first we want to discuss a point that often hampers both informality **and** variety.

Traditional Seating Design

Most meeting rooms seem to be set up with chairs in rows and columns.

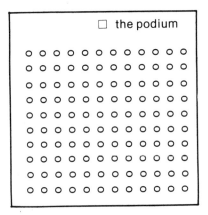

This is exactly the kind of set-up that "super leaders" want. There's no question about who's in charge, and it's even better if the podium is on a riser so everyone can see the "important one." It works fine when the members are listening to a speaker or looking at material projected on a screen, but it doesn't do much for the membership when you want them to discuss a matter informally.

"Rows and columns" is a rather dehumanizing situation. First, nonverbal communication among the members is eliminated (who **ever** gets an indication of how another person is feeling from the back of the head?). Second, people who arrive late are more likely to stand along the back wall or pick a seat at the back than they are to embarrass themselves by making an effort to find a chair. It never fails that in an almost full room the only empty seats are always in the middle of the row, and usually way up front.) Third, it's disruptive when people try to communicate with others who are either to the side, behind or in front of them. And finally, the chair in the "rows and columns" setting can choose to overlook comments from the members if he/she opts to do so; with a microphone, he/she can drown them out easily.

This may be an exaggeration of what happens when the seating is thus arranged, but it **is** intimidating and can be counter-productive. So, before automatically allowing a room to be set up in this manner, you'll want to give some thought to the possible consequences of using this setting: resentment of power, alienation from fellow members, lack of spontaneous feedback, loss of "the back wall people" (who would rather leave than have to stand up or be embarrassed), limited communication between the members and from the members to the chair, or disruption of the meeting to obtain a seat up front. It is not a design that will enable the officers to become more aware of the needs and interests of the members; it is a setting in which the members have no choice but to become more aware of the needs and interests of the officers.

One way to overcome this and to start informal discussions is simply to ask the membership to form into groups and start talking. We'd like to suggest an even better way.

Buzz Groups[1]

Have you ever noticed that people who come to a meeting together also sit together? Also, people who come to a meeting together and who sit together tend to think alike, and to agree on most things.

---

1. Material on "Buzz Groups" and "Brainstorming" adapted from Sutherland, Sidney S., *When You Preside*. Danville, Ill.: The Interstate Printers & Publishers, Inc., 1969, pp. 26-31 and 44-49. Used with permission.

By arranging members into small groups, you get people who feel one way mixed in with people who hold different opinions. In mixed groups members will sharpen each others' wits simply because they are no longer with their little clique of friends who all think alike. So be sure to arrange the group so that it is made up of people with different ideas and values. This has a good chance of becoming a productive group, and it will give the membership some variety, some new acquaintances.

How can this be done? Simply by rearranging chairs from rows to small circles. If the members are already assembled, just walk right over to a column and, with accompanying hand gestures, say, "The first five people in this column will be group #1, and the last six will be group #2," etc. Arrange them into the smallest possible circles if chairs can be moved; otherwise form clusters within the columns. In any case, walk right over there and help them do it, or have the other officers help you.

Small circles provide the best possible arrangement for people to interact, both verbally and nonverbally. You can see people's faces, experience their expressions, and respond to their feelings as well as to their words.

If the group is small, the atmosphere will be one of openness, and you can say what you feel without fear of embarrassment. Information, ideas and feedback will flow easily and total participation is almost assured. Consensus will come more easily, too. Mathematically, if there are 100 people in the room in groups of five, 20 people will be talking at the same time, and close to 100 will be actively participating. With rows and columns, only one person can talk and 99 are "just there" in various states of involvement and consciousness.

Using Buzz Groups

Buzz groups need to be told what to do, **before** you form them. Once small groups are formed, you'll literally lose control of the meeting temporarily due to people moving around and talking. So . . .

- Tell them what they are to do. "When you get into your groups, you are to come up with three **best** ways for our club to raise $1,000 between now and December 13."
- Tell them how much time they have to do it.
- Tell them to select a person to summarize their key points and report for the group.
- Then, form your buzz groups.

A word of caution! In a large group, be sure you have a microphone and speaker system to regain control of the meeting when you need it; the level of conversational noise will be a new experience for you the first time you try it.

Buzz groups have proved to be very effective for a number of common situations at meetings:

- **Converting Goals into Ideas for Action**
  Boy Scout troop #5 has as one of its continuing goals: "To make our community a safer place to live." The problem is, specifically, what shall they do this year? If you were the scoutmaster, you could form buzz groups and ask them to brainstorm every possible idea of what the troop can do this year to help make the community a safer place to live. You could follow the brainstorming procedures explained below, and then read Chapter 6 for some ideas on how to develop a specific plan of action.

- **Making Decisions**
  A Junior Chamber of Commerce of 35 members has a surplus of $200 to spend, and four alternatives have been suggested by an ad-hoc committee:
  - a. Donate it all to a local charity.
  - b. Put it in a membership loan fund.
  - c. Beautify the neighborhood park.
  - d. Have a Memorial Day barbeque for their families.

  Since, as an officer, you'd want everybody involved in making this decision, you should get a motion passed for an informal discussion and form buzz groups. Ask for a consensus from each group and have a spokesman report the outcome to the chair. If there are differences among the reports, select a member to speak for each of the alternatives still being considered and have a vote by secret ballot. Everyone will have had his say and the secret ballot will prevent peer pressure in voting.

- **Evaluating a Meeting or Event**
  Buzz groups with consensus on the best ideas for improving the next meeting will have involved everybody, and the evaluation task can be over in 10 minutes.

- **Nominating Officers**
  Explain the qualifications necessary for each officer, then form buzz groups to discuss members who are most qualified. Check them out to be sure they are interested, and the actual nomination can come from any member in the group.

- **Selecting Activities**
  Buzz groups and brainstorming are excellent methods for deciding the details of the annual reunion, an open house, a money-raising activity, the program for the next meeting . . . there's no limit to the applications.

- **Interacting with Speakers**
  Whenever it is planned to give members an opportunity to interact with a speaker, a committee chairman giving a committee report, debaters or several speakers on a panel, buzz groups can be very effective.

  Everybody can get involved in analyzing what the speaker(s) said and the questions written by a representative of the buzz group's discussion are likely to be of better quality than questions posed by individuals. This process virtually eliminates the likelihood that some "big mouth" will take this opportunity to capture the spotlight to ask an embarrassing or inappropriate question.

  Another possibility is to have the speakers visit briefly with buzz groups, on invitation, to give information and answer questions. Visiting speakers will enjoy this more than sitting on the stage, waiting to see what is going to happen next. When the speakers have finished visiting among the buzz groups, ask them to return to the front and make any concluding remarks, and to receive the applause of appreciation from your entire membership.

If the situation involves a complex committee report, or one of special importance, the members of the committee can visit buzz groups to give information and answer questions. When all buzz groups have been satisfied, you should call the meeting back to order and ask, "Do I hear a motion?"

- **Recess and After the Meeting**

Buzz groups are very effective for getting a group together during a recess, or for keeping a committee together after the meeting. These little meetings are often very important and too often they are done standing around in a hallway where there are many distractions. Groups will accomplish more in less time if they will sit down in a little tight circle where they can give the topic total concentration.

Brainstorming Ideas [2]

Brainstorming is an excellent process for encouraging spontaneity, and getting imaginative ideas from your members in an environment void of judgment or censure. It works well using buzz groups. There should be at least five or six people involved in each group, but, if need be, this method can also be used in groups as large as 20 or 25.

Five basic rules must be rigidly observed when you brainstorm, and it's important to make them very clear at the outset:

1. Every idea presented must be positive.
2. Every idea should be stated briefly.
3. No comments will be allowed on any idea presented. Criticism of ideas presented is absolutely forbidden.

---

2. Material on "Buzz Groups" and "Brainstorming" adapted from Sutherland, Sidney S., *When You Preside*. Danville, Ill.: The Interstate Printers & Publishers, Inc., 1969, pp. 26-31 and 44-49. Used with permission.

4. Everyone is encouraged to speak up and to express ideas regardless of how fantastic they may seem.
5. Everyone is encouraged to present ideas as rapidly as they come to mind.

When all ideas have been listed (or your allotted time is up) the originator of each idea explains it in more detail. After all ideas are fully explained, the group selects the best (in priority order) by voting, and the most popular are considered for adoption by the entire membership.

The Personal Agenda

The personal agenda gives all members the opportunity to speak to the entire group about their concerns and priorities. Most people **do** like to talk . . . to hear themselves. This process gives them a **license** to talk . . . and they enjoy it! It is an effective tool to use to determine the interests of the members, whether new or old. It gives everybody the experience of discovering the items that have high priority among the entire membership. The ideal group size is about 15, although it may be used with groups as large as 30 by shortening the time given each individual to "do his thing."

Here's how to do it:
A. Arrange the group in a circle with everyone facing the center.
B. Inform the group that each person will be given the opportunity to do **one** of three things:
  - **Ask a question to get factual information:**
    "Where can I buy a good pair of hiking boots in this town?"
  - **Ask for help in solving a problem:**
    "My kayak has a two-foot hole in its bottom, and I need to know how to fix it."
  - **Make a statement:**
    "I think we are ignoring the needs of new members and

I, for one, bla . . . bla . . . bla."
Make it clear that participants must choose to do only one of the above and that they will be given only two or three minutes in which to pose their question, or make their statement, and receive feedback from the group. When the group begins giving feedback, individuals should be prepared to take notes on the information or help they receive.

C. Begin with any person who is ready with an item, and call "time" at the end of each person's three minutes.

D. Repeat the process until everyone in the group has had an opportunity to speak.

The personal agenda gives everyone in the group two good experiences: that of being helped by others in the group and that of helping others by sharing with them information which the others may not have access to or experience with. And it gives the officers a chance to really listen to those issues that are of major concern to the general membership.

Note: The officers may participate in the personal agenda exercise if they wish, but they should have no more voice, power or control than the regular members. Whoever is facilitating the exercise should do just that—keep time and keep things moving! The facilitator should **not** get involved in the content of what is being said.

Your Program Committee

If you have programs along with your business meetings, the program committee can be a valuable resource for providing variety.

Good programs don't just happen; they are the result of careful planning. A good program committee can bring order, continuity and balance to the activities of an organization.

Organizations often overemphasize the importance of internal, mechanical and administrative details, and put too little effort into keeping the meetings alive, interesting and valuable to the membership! If you have delegated sufficient authority to the executive committee and they have handled the hard-core "administrivia," the program committee will have more time for relevant, "growthy," or just plain fun activities.

Program committee members can come from anywhere within the organization: the only requisites for participation should be enthusiasm, a willingness to experiment, sensitivity to the needs of other members, and commitment to providing many different kinds of activities.

When planning activities, committee members should keep in mind that all good programs must:

- Reflect the objectives of the organization.
- Respond to the diversity of interests within the membership.
- Start and end on time.
- Make provisions for fellowship.
- Encourage members to do things they may not have tried before.
- Provide for physical comfort.
- Add something to each person's life.

Too often, program committees get hung up on trivia and lose sight of their importance to the organization. Here are some guidlines for what **NOT** to do:

- Include a program just because "we did it last year."
- Give too much importance to getting "big name" celebrities and people with titles.
- Overplay entertainment.
- Let the program chairman do it all alone.
- Be afraid to try something unique, different.

So that some of these pitfalls can be avoided, here are a few suggestions:

- Form a program committee composed of your most interested and creative members who represent a wide variety of interests.
- Have an annual plan—a framework that represents a program design based upon the group's objectives and the members' interests—and keep it flexible for current events.
- Each week distribute the responsibility for programs to a different sub-group that will plan a unique program for each meeting (The organization's program chairman and committee should coordinate and assist, but they should let the sub-group take full charge.)
- Be alert to program ideas in magazines, newspapers, radio and television.

- Solicit ideas from the general membership by (this is a continuous job!):

   Conducting Interviews: Each member of the program committee takes five to ten members and interviews them by phone, or face to face. (The committee should determine beforehand what questions to ask.)

   Surveying member interests with a questionnaire.

   Brainstorming in Buzz Groups: Compile a master list, then have the program committee consider all ideas and prepare a monthly, quarterly or annual program for group approval.

The program committee of any organization should be among the busiest, most enthusiastic and most innovative of all existing sub-groups.

Be sure your program committee prepares a complete annual report and participates in the year-end transfer between old and new officers, as described in Chapter 9.

Meetings that are organized, flexible and filled with variety will help keep your members interested and coming back for more, but many organizations don't meet weekly (or even monthly). Chapter 6 will be of particular interest to those of you who want to improve the quality of the organizational business that must be transacted between meetings, whether they are weekly or just once a year.

Meetings are peaks
In the life of a club,
But the days in between
We usually flub.

Rise out of those valleys!
Build bridges across!
Make time between meetings
More profit than loss.

CHAPTER 6

Bridging the
Between-Meetings Gap

Let's assume that you 1) had a terrific first meeting of the year, 2) can run a dynamic standard business meeting, and 3) have a highly competent secretary who writes beautiful minutes.

Is there anything more you can do to make your organization more effective? YES! You can become competent at "bridging the gap" **between** meetings.

The vigor and forward movement of an organization depends just as much on what happens between meetings as it does on what happens at the meetings themselves. Many organizations just **vegetate** between meetings. When there is little or no follow up to the decisions made at the previous general meeting, you're likely to hear "no report" when called for the next time your organization meets.

The Team

There's nothing like a team of fellow officers and hard-core workers to keep the organization moving between meetings. So if each team member has some assigned follow up projects, you'll see greater progress. Form a team of the most committed and reliable members . . . the newsletter editor, the bulletin board coordinator, the secretary, a hard-working member "without portfolio," all your committee chairpersons and the other officers. Have some team social activities as well as between-meeting planning and work sessions. Have some fun together . . . get to know one another through such events as progressive dinners, a day at the lake, pot lucks in each others' homes or apartments, lunch with a few people at a time.

Occasionally, do some project planning together, and keep in touch with each others' progress on and problems with their respective projects. Help one another and use the telephone frequently. It's a good feeling to get a call from the president, "Hi, Fred. How are you doing on that "toys-for-tots" project? Need any help?"

Write a team letter regularly when your team lives in places that are widely dispersed through a district or region. It keeps them in touch with what's going on between meetings and among themselves so they don't feel all alone "out there." Use the telephone; try a conference call to get some needed interaction or to discuss items of special importance. You'll find more information elsewhere in this Chapter on newsletters, telephones and bulletin boards.

Hold a team (or executive committee) meeting to pull things together before the next general meeting. Finalize the agenda and decide the role and readiness of each person taking part in the meeting.

Committees Can Help

A great deal of an organization's between-meeting achievement depends upon the careful selection of committee members and chairpersons, and upon the effective functioning of these committees.

Individual committees have several advantages over the organization as a whole. A small group can consider, plan and carry out an assignment more efficiently than a large, unwieldly organization. It can meet more often, deliberate more completely, and work more rapidly than the entire organization. Members have the opportunity to become "expert" in their task.

There is greater freedom of discussion, more informal procedures may be followed, and delicate, troublesome or embarrassing questions are more easily handled.

They may hold hearings and call upon "outsiders" to bring more expert or objective information into the situation.

Committees are called by many names, the most common being standing, ad hoc and task force. A committee is simply a sub-group of an organization that is given a specific task to do. Committees may be formed to plan a program, implement a group goal, study an issue in depth, gather facts on which to base a decision, or manage a single aspect of the organization (such as finances).

- **A standing committee** continues year after year. It's named in the organization's bylaws and can manage such affairs as finance, membership, programs or publicity. (Later we'll discuss two of these in detail to give you a guideline for committee procedures.)

- **An ad hoc committee** is a special committee which is formed to meet specific short-term organizational needs, such as fact-finding or planning a special event. Ad hoc committees make recommendations to the general membership.

- **A task force** is an ad hoc committee with power and authority to take action on an assigned problem; it is not a recommending body and its membership is accountable for whatever action is taken. A task force can be appointed either by the organization (to take action on a matter before the next meeting), or it may be appointed by a higher authority (to take action as a sub-unit of a larger organization, such as a local chapter of a national organization).

Selecting and Instructing Committees

The selection of the committee chairperson can be the key to
its success or failure and for this reason, the **process** of
selection is critical.

- Be sure the total membership understands the goal of the
  committee **before** the chair is selected.
- Be sure that the membership participates in the selection of
  the committee chairperson by offering suggestions to the
  chair, in the case of an appointive position, by election.
- Be sure that the method of selection of the chair conveys an
  attitude of importance or prestige. **Don't** ask for a volunteer
  without the benefit of an adequate discussion of what will
  be expected.

Have you ever heard a presiding officer ask, "We're looking
for a volunteer to be chairperson of the awards banquet. You
don't need any special talent or experience and you can do just
about anything you want to do. I'm sure it won't take much time.
Anyone interested?" The most likely thing about this approach
is that you are likely to get a loser. In general, a potential
chairperson should have the following qualifications:

- Be able to lead discussions and coordinate ideas and the
  use of energy.
- Understand the committee assignment and be committed to
  it.
- Have the knowledge and experience necessary for the task
  to be done.
- Be willing to devote the necessary time to the assignment.

And, although selection of committee members may not seem
as crucial as choosing the right chairperson, there are some
essential qualities that members should possess and certain
considerations they should be able to expect from the
organization.

They must:

- Feel that the work of the committee is important.
- Feel that the organization will pay attention to the
  committee's report and implement the committee's recommendations.
- Feel a sense of participation and belonging.

Once a committee has been elected or appointed, it is your responsibility (with the help of the membership) to give the committee specific instructions about its task, and to give it some tools with which to work. These include:

- A clear statement of the problem, including the limits of authority.
- A list of the names and phone numbers of the committee chairperson and all the members.
- Necessary resource materials (e.g.; constitution or bylaws, policies, past records, reports).
- Suggestions from the membership on possible committee methods and resources.
- The date the report is due and the form it should take.

You may want to read again some of the techniques mentioned in Chapter 5, such as buzz groups, brainstorming and interest inventories.

Action-Oriented Committee Reports

A committee report is usually supervised by the chairperson and written in collaboration with the members. The general character of the report is necessarily guided by the nature of the committee's assignment, but even brief reports should be submitted in writing for the record and the minutes. Important reports are generally reproduced and distributed to every member. When this is done, a summary of the full report is read at the meeting. The entire report should be filed with the secretary and a summary included in the minutes.

Every committee report should include these five main points:

1. A statement of the motion or assignment which was referred to the committee.
2. A statement of what the committee is expected to do with the assignment; that is, take action, make recommendations, fact-find, clarify or investigate.
3. A brief summary of the methods used by the committee, that is, the general plan.
4. The information gathered or a summary of work accomplished.

5. Conclusions, findings, recommendations or resolutions.

There are seven possible actions an organization can take on a committee report. The action taken should be stated in the minutes:

It can be:	This means it has been:
FILED	Received and included in the organization's records without opinion or action.
POSTPONED	Postponed to a more convenient or appropriate time.
RETURNED	Given back or re-referred to the committee for more information or work.
ADOPTED	Accepted by the organization including any opinions, conclusions, recommendations, or resolutions which are in the report.
DIVIDED ADOPT	Divided in order to accept parts of the report and not accept other parts.
REFERRED	Referred to an officer, another committee or the board of directors for further study and recommendation.
SUBSTITUTED	Rejected in favor of a minority report.

Two Basic Standing Committees

After all this talk about different kinds of committees, member selection, and committee functions, we thought it would be helpful to give examples of two relatively common standing committees: the executive committee and the publicity committee. Both are typical of the kinds of standing committees that exist within organizations, and both have important responsibilities to fulfill. Because there are as many different kinds of committees as there are different interests within groups, we thought it best to simply mention two whose procedures and processes can be fairly easily generalized to meet your specific needs.

The Executive Committee

The executive committee is usually made up of the officers, standing committee chairpeople and frequently other significant individuals as dictated by the activities and functions of the organization. Its fundamental purpose is to serve as a clearing house for all organizational problems. Its duties may include such things as:

- Coordination of organizational activities within the organization itself or in conjunction with other groups.
- Acting for the entire membership in times of emergency.
- Problem identification involving potentially troublesome issues and situations.
- Taking official action as required by the bylaws or constitution.

As can be inferred by glancing at this list of possible "XCOM" (Executive Committee) functions, a committee of this kind is most helpful in large organizations, or in groups with widely-varied interests or programs. And, although the frequency of XCOM meetings will depend upon the volume and breadth of the organization's business and the efficiency of its officers, many groups find it helpful to have the XCOM take charge of preparation for each regular meeting of the group.

Here are some ideas for the full utilization of the resources of your executive committee:

- Help them become thoroughly informed about the organization's constitution, objectives and traditions. These items should be fully discussed at its first meeting of the year.
- Ask the vice-president to take a great deal of responsibility for the XCOM. Some organizations have the vice-president chair this group, and the president presides over general meetings.
- Instill a sense of teamwork within the XCOM. Members should be encouraged to support one another with ideas and assistance on specific assignments.
- Insist that the XCOM accept the responsibility and authority it deserves as stated in the bylaws.
- Discuss important business in XCOM before it is brought up

at a general meeting. Be sure this important group understands the problems, alternatives and consequences before the business is presented to the general meeting.

- Try to get the XCOM to develop various alternatives and prepare checklists, panel discussions, role playing, etc., to stimulate general membership involvement in the ultimate decision. Have them become a part of different buzz groups whenever you form small groups for discussion.
- Have XCOM handle routine, minor business between meetings. This will keep the general meeting from getting cluttered up and it will give the membership more time for the important issues.

The possibilities of an XCOM are endless. Its members are, after all, the "cream of the membership crop." Be wary, though, of the power such a group can wield—never allow it to become so strong, so efficient or so autonomous that the general membership feels left out of the decision-making process.

The Publicity Committee

There are times when your organization will want to inform the public about its activities, or get a large number of people to attend one of its events. No matter how well a program for the public may be planned, its chances of being an unqualified success depends upon your publicity being timely, appealing and convincing.

Publicity can be defined as the ways you intentionally or UNintentionally reach the various groups of persons you have reason to believe will be of service to you through their efforts or attendance.

Effective publicity takes PLANNING based on **accurate** knowledge of:

- What your organization wishes to accomplish.
- The people who can do the most to help you, or those who might prevent you from achieving your organizational goals.
- What is most likely to interest those people in you.
- The most effective ways of reaching them at times when they can be of greatest service.

Effective publicity takes work over an extended period of time. It is part of a planned program and involves regular preparation and regular follow-through. Much of publicity's most productive efforts are cumulative—the publicity you use this week will secure results, in many instances, from the publicity you have produced in the past. For this reason, a good publicity committee should include some of the hardest-working, most dedicated persons in the organization.

Publicity's results are determined not by the amount of comment you hear, or the praises you receive for your work, but by the actual accomplishment of selected goals—increasing membership or attendance, producing greater willingness of competent persons to serve as officers or committee personnel, etc. You cannot measure the effectiveness of publicity unless you have specific objectives.

An efficient publicity person will make a study of all possible publicity media available. Here are some possibilities:

- Daily/weekly newspapers (go to the news editor, introduce yourself, and learn how to prepare your story and photos, meet deadlines, etc.).
- Local radio and television stations (public service announcements or commercial "spots").
- Publications of groups with interests similar to yours.
- Flyers, pamphlets, banners, posters.
- Downtown store windows.

You must have a "live organization" if you expect to develop "live publicity," and both your organization and its publicity must depend for their real success on constructive service to the genuine interests of the people you wish to reach and influence.

Effective committee work will help bridge the gap between meetings and move the organization along the road to accomplishing its goals. But the general membership needs to be kept informed of all this work and progress if you are to keep their interest in the organization at a high level.

How can you keep everybody informed? It isn't easy when you may not see each other for weeks or months at a time. For this specific situation, there's nothing like distributing a newsletter, getting on the phone, or keeping members up to date by means of a well-placed and lively bulletin board.

Newsletters. Newsletters offer an excellent means of letting members know "What's happening" in an interesting way. Here are some ideas:
- Give a calendar of coming events.
- Name people who are doing important work for the organization.
- Outline recent decisions that affect the organization, internal and external.
- Use cartoons and free-hand lettering and art work; they offer variety and are eye-catchers.
- Identify new members.
- Portray personalities.
- Promote group's projects.
- Sharpen objectives.

Telephones. When something important is coming up, use the telephone! Have you ever tried a telephone-chain? It's easy to do. Simply divide the membership into groups of about 10 and organize a group of your most committed members to phone "their 10" when it's important. Since each telephone volunteer has 10 people to contact, the telephone chain doesn't overload anyone, and it is fast.

Bulletin Boards. If you're lucky enough to have a building or central place where your members visit or pass in their daily or weekly routines, try a bulletin board! A bulletin board can serve as a unique vehicle for getting information to the membership. Photographs, brochures and magazine cut-outs can be displayed; timely information can be posted without delay; notes can be written between members, and interested persons can be encouraged to become prospective members.

Newsletters, the telephone, and bulletin boards should all be a part of a well-rounded publicity program.

It's not enough to be expert at conducting organizational meetings. Much of the real work must be done between meetings, or group progress will be seriously jeopardized. For this reason, leaders need to brush up on those skills that pertain to: 1) selecting and working with committees, 2) writing and processing committee reports, 3) using an executive committee wisely, and 4) developing effective publicity and between-meeting communications.

With a little time and effort and with the help of your officers and members, you'll soon be able to effectively bridge the gap between meetings. Then you'll really be ready to move on to bigger and better things, like goal setting, problem solving, elections and evaluation. These processes are the heart of organizational life, and you can read **all** about them in the chapters that follow.

A goal is like a cherished dream
We hope will soon come true
It takes the efforts of the group
Not those of just a few.

So imagine to your hearts' content
And set some mighty goals
Then draft a plan of action, please,
In which there are no holes.

CHAPTER 7

Goal Setting:
Making Dreams Come True

Hopes are often built on dreams. Similarly, the goals you establish are dreams that can come true and bring you and your organization a sense of success, accomplishment and pride.

As a culture, we respect those who attain their goals. We also tend to enjoy vicariously the total experience of those who win or achieve. We see this in the poems and stories we read, in the songs we sing, and in the events we attend or watch on television. And yet, despite the public's love affair with success and happiness, many of us choose not to take part—not to "play the game." Instilled in many of us is the fear of failure or the fear of inadequacy. This is a sad but true commentary on the time in which we live.

People who have become members of organizations have taken a big step out of the passive role of a spectator and are saying, "I want to get involved; I want to be part of the action."

That's what this chapter is all about . . . how to convert dreams into goals and goals into plans of action.

Since **Leadership Is . . . Everybody's Business**, the primary source of goals is the membership of the group. What are their interests, concerns and dreams? An interest inventory . . . (See

Exercise 9, Chapter 3) and buzz group brainstorming . . . (See Chapter 5) might be productive techniques to use to get every member's ideas out in the open, and give them an opportunity to talk about them. They also help to provide feedback from others in the smaller groups so that even though a large number of potential goals is generated, only a few of the most feasible survive the test of interaction to be recommended to the entire membership for consideration as goals and objectives of their organization.

Organizational goals do, of course, have constraints. Organizations are formed for a reason. Each has a particular mission or purpose for existing, and this is made explicit in the constitution and/or bylaws. (It isn't likely that the League of Women Voters would ever give organizational approval of a major group goal which would involve organizing and funding a bowling league!)

Organizations also have traditions that carve a path through the landscape. These very definitely give the members direction as they consider the year ahead, and are the driving forces that keep the organization "on track."

Although traditional activities will no doubt continue to hold an important place in the lives of organizations with long histories, and although they make the eyes of the alumni moist with nostalgic pride, every group should provide a reasonable beam of light for creativity and change . . . within the bylaws.

An Antidote to Apathy

Membership participation in goal-setting is the antidote to apathy. So, manage the meeting to encourage participation. Make it easy for everyone to talk . . . to participate . . . to get involved. Perhaps the most common fault of the chairperson is talking too much: prescribing what the goals should be, explaining how goals were accomplished last year, pleading with the members to volunteer, making them feel guilty if they don't volunteer, offering trophies for doing the best job.

Just let the members talk; they'll talk themselves right into a committee!

Richard Armour made this point beautifully with a little poem entitled "Don't look at me, I didn't say anything!"

"At meetings of clubs, by an effort of will,
I always contrive to keep perfectly still,
For it takes but a word of annoyance or pity,
And wham! There I am on another committee!" [1]

A Word About Motivation

Participation and involvement is the main line to a person's motivational system. "Turning a person on" is a myth. All you can do is manage the structure, atmosphere and dynamics of a meeting to give an individual the freedom and opportunity to get involved, and to anticipate meaningful outcomes that will lead him or her to further involvement. The ultimate level is commitment to a goal, and the amount of energy put forth to achieve it is each person's alone to determine, it's like getting "hooked" on your own party dip.

Images to Action Planning

"Imaging potentiality" is a unique and optimistic process developed by Fox, Lippit, and Schindler-Rainman (1973) for developing goals. [2] Basically, the process employs "images" as a way of identifying and establishing goals. It uses the past as a reference, not as the ultimate source of all ideas and directions. The key is to recognize the present situation and then "leap" into the future to create images of what could be.

There are basically six steps in the images of potentiality approach to goal setting:

---

1. From *Learning Parliamentary Procedure* by Alice F. Sturgis, p. 246. Copyright 1953 by McGraw-Hill, Inc. Used by permission of McGraw-Hill Book Company.

2. Fox, R.S., Lippitt, R., and Schindler-Rainman, E., *Toward a Humane Society: Images of Potentiality.* Fairfax, VA: National Training Laboratories Learning Resources Corporation, 1973. Used with permission.

Step I: The Fantasy Trip: Ask all members of the organization to relax totally and close their eyes. Make sure everyone really gets into this and is relaxed. Tell them they have the uncanny ability to see through time; tell them they can see change, hear conversations and see through walls. Have them imagine they are attending the final meeting of the year and that there is a discussion of this year's accomplishments. All participants, while totally relaxed, should think about what they see, hear or imagine about your organization that makes them feel good, proud and satisfied. Once everyone's had enough time to do this, (usually 5 minutes or so) ask them to list their images on the sheets of paper you have provided. Each statement should begin with the words, "I see . . . ". Plenty of time should be allotted for them to do this so that everyone can participate in the steps that follow.

Step II: Sharing: When everyone has had a chance to take a "trip" and record their images, form them into small groups of three to six persons and ask them to take turns sharing what they "saw". Interaction should be encouraged and everyone should have the opportunity to speak.

Step III: Creating Objectives: When the image-sharing experience has been completed, have each group pick a single image experience (or one image experience per person) which they feel would be a worthy goal for the organization. This image should be written in specific, clearly defined measurable terms. For instance:

- **Image Example #1:** "I see a big turnout at a religious rally."

  Refined Goal Statement: By May 20, ten thousand people will attend an all-day religious rally in the Memorial Stadium which will net $25,000 for the Slippery Pebble Community Church.

- **Image Example #2:** "I see a pile of food in a truck and it's being distributed to needy people."

Refined Goal Statement: At least 80% of the membership will volunteer three hours on Saturday, November 15 to collect a total of one ton of canned goods for the Salvation Army.

- **Image Example #3:** "I see a successful 'rush' during the fall semester."

  Refined Goal Statement: By September 15, Alpha Beta Gamma will have 15 pledges with grade point averages of 3.0 or above.

- **Image Example #4:** "I see a lot of people attending a show in the art gallery."

  Refined Goal Statement: At least 6,000 people will attend the two-week-long annual Pottery Show; of those attending, 1,500 people will make positive comments in the art gallery register about the show.

- **Image Example #5:** "I see a successful church bazaar."

  Refined Goal Statement: By October 15, at least 60 people will be signed up to donate something for the annual church bazaar.

Step IV: Positive and Negative Forces: At this point, the most popular, highest-priority goal from all those suggested is selected and analyzed. Ask each group to write down the positive factors in the environment which can help influence the achievement of the goal. Then have them list all the barriers or difficulties that must be faced and overcome in the process of achieving the goal. This takes time, but if taken seriously, time will actually be saved as you begin to move ahead with your planning.

Here's an example of Step IV. Suppose that when you analyze the first refined goal statement of "By May 20, ten thousand people will attend an all-day religious rally in the Memorial Stadium which will net $25,000 for the Slippery Pebble Community Church." The results may turn out like this:

NEGATIVE FACTORS	POSITIVE FACTORS
1. The electrical capacity of the stadium will not provide the power needed.	1. The people in the community are ready for a religious rally.
2. The manager of the stadium will not permit trucks on the field.	2. The stadium will hold 10,000 people.
3. Our committee is too small to do all the work.	3. $25,000 will give us enough to purchase the additional land needed to expand facilities around the church.

Step V: Assigning Valences: Minus numbers (1 to 4) are assigned to the barriers which stand in the way of your accomplishing the goal. The lower the number, the more awesome the barrier. Let's assume that the valences assigned to each factor by the membership are:

NEGATIVE FACTORS	POSITIVE FACTORS
1. The electrical capacity of the stadium will not provide the power needed. (4)	1. The people in the community are ready for a religious rally. (3)
2. The manager of the stadium will not permit trucks on the field. (2)	2. The stadium will hold 10,000 people. (4)
3. Our committee is too small to do all the work. (1)	3. $25,000 will give us enough to purchase the additional land needed to expand facilities around the church. (4)

You don't have to do anything with the list of positive factors. Listing them is a valuable step, however, in that it identifies friendly people, facts and resources without which you might not have the courage to go ahead. Also, organizations have been known to spend unnecessary time working on making the good things better, when the negative factors are the things that **really** remain in the way of attaining the goal. It would do little good, for example, for the Slippery Pebble Community Church folks to establish a committee to increase the readiness of the community for the event or to make the stadium more attractive. What if they did? They still wouldn't have solved any of the negative factors which are preventing them from having a religious rally.

Step VI: Overcoming the Barriers: It's time to chip away at the identifiable barriers related to the selected goal, beginning with the most simple and working up to the more difficult ones. Some groups prefer to attempt to overcome the more difficult barriers first and then work down to the less difficult ones, but for most volunteer groups, it is helpful to build success upon success rather than stumble over a task that proves to be too difficult. Therefore, we suggest that you take on the easy ones first, and as your confidence gets stronger and stronger, the more difficult obstacles won't seem quite so intimidating. Finding solutions for the negative factors can be done through brainstorming (See Chapter 5) and your results become plans for action.

Imaging potentialities is not a simple or quick process; things that are done democratically are seldom quick. But, since both goalsetting and developing plans of action are truly everybody's business, it will take time and involvement from everyone to get the job done. As you become more and more experienced with using this process, the results themselves will convince you that it's worth the effort. When each barrier can be obliterated by a plan of action that has been developed by the total membership, commitment will be strong and goals will be reached.

Solving problems is like a voyage
On a ship that rocks to and fro.
Just hold on tight, and forge ahead,
And soon you'll reach your goal.

It takes the crew, together
With each one doing a part
A team to sail the tradewinds
To that goal upon their chart.

CHAPTER 8

Problem Solving
and Decision Making

Making decisions about setting goals by means of imaging (Chapter 7) is the most effective way we know of putting together an annual program of organizational objectives. Imaging the future (by looking back) early in the year when hopes are high, with total membership involvement, gives great promise for a successful year. It is a long-range matter; there is no immediate problem as such, and you can take your time. Goal-setting is simply a response to the question, "What shall we do?" referring to possible projects and programs. In athletics, this would be called a "game plan".

Knowing how to solve a problem, on the other hand, becomes an important issue when something unforeseen develops which must be resolved quickly, within a definite time frame. This is a common occurrence in groups that don't plan ahead, but it can also happen in groups that have done a great deal of planning.

Although there are many reasons for poor decision making in problem-solving situations, two stand out among all the others:

1. **Lack of time**—membership involvement takes time, and membership involvement is essential to quality decision making and to member commitment to a decision. One way

to avoid this particular pitfall of poor decision making is to **plan ahead** . . . anticipate problems that may develop, keep "on "top" of projects and programs. The second way is, simply, to **take the time.** It may require a couple of extra meetings and/or special committee work to overcome the dilemma. Either you must take the time from other priorities to reach high-quality decisions or face the consequences of developing a poorly-conceived solution. Very often you can't affort **not** to take the time.

2. **Lack of skills** in decision making—In this chapter we'll present a process made up of several logical and systematic steps that can lead to a good, solid decision. This process didn't occur to us spontaneously, while in the midst of making a crisis decision; it's a result of many years of observation and practical application. We think this concept of decision making can be used to handle major problems regardless of the group or the situation. First we'll present the problem solving process diagramatically, and then we'll give you a true-life example of how a typical organization might implement the various steps.

Step I: Defining the Problem. Step I is the most crucial step of all. If the problem is not adequately defined in terms that everyone can understand, confusion about the problem will stymie progress towards a solution throughout the entire process. An exercise that is designed to assist small and large groups alike in accurately defining a problem is the "Problem -Solving Triad" at the end of this chapter. Keep in mind (especially with large groups) that much time can be saved if the problem is presented visually. Use various audio-visual aids such as chalkboards, video taping, overhead projectors and easels. Be sure to relate the problem to the organization's goals.

Step II: Knowing the Team. In order to arrive at a quality solution (one which will have maximum support from the membership), it is essential that the organization be fully aware of its resources and talent: i.e.; you must discover the uniqueness of the individuals within your organization. There are numerous activities and exercises which can be used to do just this. (See Exercises 2-9, Chapter 3.)

The Process of Effective Problem Solving and Decision Making

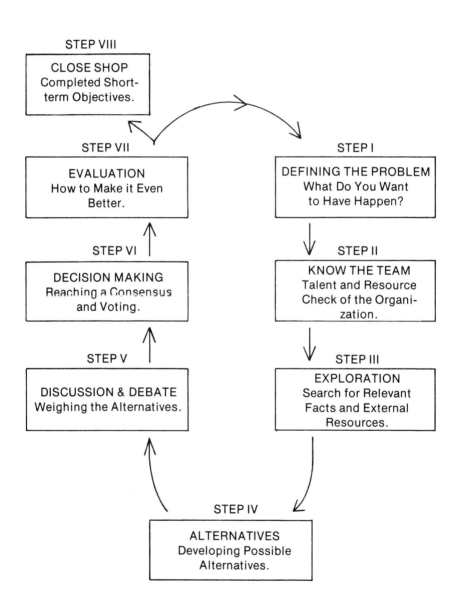

The interest inventory in particular (Exercise 9, Chapter 3) is a good start, and it does make available important information about members. An Organizational Resource Information Card can also be used to acquaint officers with member interests and skills, to assist them in problem solving and decision making, or to form standing or special committees. A sample card is shown at the end of this chapter. For the best results, distribute it to all members at the first official business meeting of the year.

Don't expect a one- or two-hour meeting to be sufficient time to transact business **and** get to know the membership. Plan some socials, retreats or workshops to help the members get better acquainted and to identify resources BEFORE you begin solving major problems, setting goals and delineating objectives.

Step III: Exploration. First, determine what facts are known by the membership, using brainstorming or small groups (See Chapter 5). Checklists and fact-finding teams can be helpful in this regard.

• **Using Checklists:** At this point it might be advantageous to look at the value a checklist can provide your organization. The checklist offers numerous alternatives for the organization, each one of them a plausible solution. Having the members check off their first, second and third choices causes each individual to think more about the problem rather than to respond emotionally. In a very explicit way, it commits the member to favor certain alternatives over others.

Remember that a checklist is **not** a ballot. It is **not** a final decision. Rather, it is a beginning point for the entire membership. A checklist differs from an agenda, discussion outline or other method of stimulating discussion in that it alone requires each member to make a personal, overt choice-commitment that tends to prepare that member psychologically for involvement in the discussion which will follow Some typical situations for use of discussion-stimulating checklists are:

• How can the Knights of Columbus earn $1,000 during the year for the County Charity Relief Fund?
• What action shall Signa Phi take against the treasurer who embezzled $300?

- How can the P.T.A. double its membership?
- What emblem shall the F.F.A. choose for its new logo?
- How can the students of California Polytechnic State University best spend their activity fees?

- **Fact-finding:** It should never be assumed that the best or only solution to a problem will be found **solely** within the membership. Despite the vast resources of your members, look beyond your organization for help when it is clear that extending your search for facts will improve your understanding of the situation; become aware of all environmental sources of information.

There are numerous ways to "fact-find" or gather information. Here are some standard sources and methods of procuring reliable facts and information.

1. **Authorities:** (Experts) Two or three are better than one. Select them from different philosophies or allegiances. (A wise man once said, "When you have a committee of 10 who all think alike, get rid of nine of them.")

2. **Documents:** Bylaws, codes, policies, minutes, agreements, contracts, earlier studies, methods or ideas. Are there any clues from current written policy, or have other groups with a similar problem employed an idea which could fit your organization's needs?

3. **Publications:** Reference books. Avoid accepting a single authority or author.

4. **General Election/Vote:** A traditional way of obtaining popular opinion. Its validity is limited to the opinion, judgment or will of those voting, but it is nevertheless an indicator.

5. **Surveys:**
   - **Questionnaires:** Design them to be brief, clear and easy to score. Consider scoring by mark-sense equipment, IBM cards or boxes along the margin. Get design help from experts. Run a pilot tryout on at least 10 people (not the committee in #1, please!) before deciding on a final format.

- **Questionnaire-Interviews:** An adaptation of the above with the interviewer filling in the answers. This procedure increases uniformity of responses when the interviewer is trained in the interviewing techniques, and is objective and non-partisan.
- **Questionnaire-Mailing:** A preliminary letter with a pre-addressed postcard commitment often gets a larger eventual return than sending a bulky questionnaire initially. Offer to send a report of the results to those who participate in the survey.
- **Sampling:** Random samples only. Use table of random numbers, data processing cards or some directory system of selecting names . . . every 20th card or name, or some number-sequence determined in advance. In all cases, the first card or name should be selected randomly.

Warning: In attempting to accumulate information on which to base alternatives, try not to let personal opinions and individual biases limit the fact-finding procedure.

Step IV: Alternatives. Once the members are satisfied that they have collected all available internal and external facts and information, it's time to develop several alternative plans of action. Open up all possible avenues that may lead to a solution.

There are three basic rules for developing these alternatives:
1. There must be a commitment to conduct an exhaustive search for all plausible alternatives.
2. There must be an absence of bias and premature commitment.
3. There must be an absence of premature criticism of alternatives.

Step V: Discussion and Debate. Weigh the alternatives and discuss the pro's and con's of each. Let members amend and combine alternatives before a final decision is reached. To make the most of this situation during your meeting, we recommend the following procedure:

1. Present the alternatives for all to see by using a chalkboard, easel or overhead projector.
2. Encourage questions about or qualifications (perhaps justifications) of the alternatives so that the entire organization understands them fully.
3. Divide the membership into buzz groups. (A mixture of ideas and backgrounds make the most productive groups. (See Chapter 5.)
4. Solicit a spokesman to present each alternative to the total membership.
5. Give each spokesman a defined amount of time.
6. Allow the buzz groups adequate time to discuss the various alternatives once the presentations have been made. During this time, the spokesman should be prepared to answer questions upon the request of individual buzz groups.
7. Have someone from each buzz group report the overall feeling of their group back to the organization.

Step VI: Decision-Making. If the preceding steps have been followed closely, Step VI will fall right into place. The goal of the decision is a general consensus based on the full utilization of all resources and the resolution of any organizational or personal conflicts. **Consensus** is defined as reaching a decision that all members of the organization can support to some extent. And, since all reasonable alternatives have been fully explored and challenged, there will be no overt opposition to a consensus. Consensus is not easy to reach, and the decision made will not always meet with **complete** and **total** support. The key to a consensus is that there will be no "losers," "winners," hard feelings or open opposition to the decision once it is reached. Because of this, consensus is preferable to both compromise or simple voting when making important decisions that require substantial member support.

Jay Hall (1971) offers the following guidelines for reaching consensus: [1]

1. From Hall, Jay, "Decisions, Decisions, Decisions," *Psychology Today*, November, 1971, pp. 51-54. Copyright 1971 Ziff-Davis Publishing Company. Reprinted by permission of *Psychology Today* magazine.

- Avoid arguing for your own rankings (priorities). Present your position as lucidly and logically as possible, but listen to the other members' reactions and consider them carefully before you press your point.
- Do not assume that someone must win and someone must lose when discussion reaches a stalemate. Instead, look for the **next** most acceptable alternative for all parties.
- Do not change your mind simply to avoid conflict and to reach agreement and harmony. When agreement seems to come too quickly and easily, be suspicious. Explore the reasons and be sure everyone accepts the solution for basically similar or complementary reasons. Yield only to positions that have objective and logically sound foundations.
- Avoid conflict-reducing techniques such as majority vote, averages, coin-flips and bargaining. When a dissenting member finally agrees, don't feel that he must be rewarded by having his own way on some later point.
- Differences of opinion are natural and expected. Seek them out and try to involve everyone in the decision process. Disagreements can help the group's decision because with a wide range of information and opinions, there is a greater chance that the group will hit upon more adequate solutions.

Once the small consensus-seeking groups seem to be nearing agreement, a spokesman for each group should give the chairperson a number count of how many members are in favor of each of the alternatives. The chair can then call the meeting back to order and ask for a motion and a second, and the official vote can then be taken for the record. The decision is made!

Step VII: Evaluation. Since Chapter 10 is devoted entirely to the process of evaluation, it will suffice to say at this point that evaluation is the most commonly overlooked step in problem solving. After all the energies of the organization have been channeled into making the decision, and the decision has been carried into action, the usual thing is for everyone to collapse until the next meeting. The evaluation session is either not attended at all or the time is spent patting one another on the back. Instead, members should make a comprehensive attempt to collect viable feedback and constructive criticism on the decision so that organizational and individual learning and growth can continue.

Step VIII: Close Shop. The problem has been solved and the whole process has been evaluated. It is time to record it in the minutes and file it under "learning experiences" or "substantial accomplishments." Even though unforeseen problems can be disruptive in the usual order of business or in the mainstream activities of the organization, they can also serve as lessons to be remembered when planning for the future. In all likelihood, the **exact** problem will never come up again, but if proper problem-solving techniques and evaluation have been employed, your organization will be ready to take on **similar** situations again with a great deal of confidence.

In concluding this discussion on problem solving and decision making, it should be emphasized that these techniques **should not be used** every time your organization has to make a decision. This process is justified only when a **major** problem arises and a decision must be made. These are ones the entire membership should play a part in solving, for in serious matters the feelings, involvement and motivation of the members must not be denied. REMEMBER: **people will support what they help to create**.

An Example of the Process: A Square Dance Dilemma

To help you better understand the phases of the problem-solving cycle, we have included an example that will carry you through each of the steps of problem solving, from beginning to end.

Step I: Defining the Problem. The purposes of the local square dance club are to acquaint members with the art of square dancing, to teach them its history, and to send members to square dancing jamborees and competitions. The national organization with which the club is affiliated has just sent an invitation to this particular organization, requesting that it send four members to the national square dance competition some 1,500 miles away. There is much enthusiasm, but how shall the trip be financed? There is a small contingency fund which has just enough money to cover the travel expenses, but if a delegation is sent, the account would be exhausted. For the rest of the year, any unexpected emergencies or new activities would be impossible to handle.

It is at this point that the organization must decide "what they want to have happen." For simplicity's sake, let's assume that this organization wants to send representatives.

The Problem: How to appropriate funds for the activity without totally destroying the club's reserves.

Step II: Getting to Know the Team. The square dance club members all seem to react somewhat favorably to the invitation and the officers decide to allow continued discussion based on the defined problem. The concerns of the members of the finance sub-committee are made known; still, there is a general feeling on the part of the membership that the invitation should be accepted. The chairperson invites all interested members to her house Sunday afternoon for a potluck dinner—a sign-up sheet is circulated. She knows that this will be an excellent opportunity to have some fun together as well as discuss the problem in small groups or on a one-to-one basis. Members will also have the opportunity to identify others' talents and resources which might provide partial alternatives for the solution of the problem. Finally, since the chairperson has some strong personal views of her own, she asks that the vice-chairperson lead all discussions of the issue until a decision is made by the membership.

Step III: Exploration. The square dance club had a fairly good turnout at their potluck supper. Those who attended had fun and discussed the problem with other members informally.

At the next regular meeting, the chairperson asks the vice-chairperson to suggest a course of action for the club in solving the problem.

As a result of having attended the potluck dinner and after having made phone calls to those who could not attend, he recommends that the membership designate four people (by name) to serve as a fact-finding committee. There is some discussion on the qualifications of these people, and based on the discussion, an additional person is added to the proposed committee. To confirm the support of the membership for this fact-finding committee, a motion is made to establish this special committee composed of these five people. They are advised that they should be ready to present their alternatives to the organization at the next regular meeting. There is some discussion, the motion is passed, and the five members accept their assignment.

Step IV: Developing Alternative Solutions. The fact-finding committee met twice between meetings. As a result of brainstorming, many interesting and creative ideas were developed. Three members of the group volunteered to investigate all the fundraising possibilities and promised to report back. The other two persons talked with members of the Chamber of Commerce, the Downtown Merchants' Association, and a City Councilman to see if they could offer any possible financial assistance or advice. Based on all the information and facts accumulated, the fact-finding committee has come to the meeting with two alternatives to present to the club. They are:

Alternative #1: Commit half of the money needed for the trip from the club treasury and present a proposal for the other half in the form of a request to the City Council.

Alternative #2: Put on a Square Dance Exhibition and barbecue in the city's memorial hall. All money raised could be used toward the expenses for the trip. If funds from the barbecue should fall short of the total financial goal, club treasury money would be used to make up the difference.

Step V: Discussion and Debate. At the next regularly scheduled meeting, "National Square Dance Jamboree: Finances" appears under "Business Items" on the agenda. The vice-chairperson calls on the fact-finding committee. In a report explaining the history of what they have done, the special committee outlines the two alternatives they have come up with and explain why, based on all available resources and related consequences, they have offered these recommendations. At this point, a motion is made to discuss the matter informally. (See Chapter 5,

Making Your Discussions Informal.) This suspends parliamentary procedure so that a more in-depth discussion can take place before a formal vote is taken. The motion is passed and the club breaks down into small groups to discuss the decision possibilities more fully. The plan of action is taking shape.

Step VI: Decision Making. The square dance club spent a considerable amount of time discussing the two alternatives, and a consensus was eventually reached. Alternative #2, holding an exhibition and barbecue, was the consensus choice.

Step VII: Evaluation. It was announced by the chair that an extensive evaluation of the fundraising activity would be held one week after the event and that a thorough report would be presented to the club membership shortly thereafter.

You may be quick to point out that all decisions are not as easy to reach as the one made by the local square dance club. That may, indeed, be true. Depending on the organization, the situation, and even the personalities involved, a number of things can develop that can create what may seem to be insurmountable barriers to solving a problem or making a consensus decision. If this is more often than not the case in your organization, allow us the luxury of repeating some key points.

Quality decisions require openness among the entire membership. You must not limit your search to discover all available human or material resources or facts. Openness should permeate the entire membership to the extent that all members of the organization will feel that they can speak freely. The atmosphere you create should not be one that produces winners and losers, but rather one that encourages team work. Perhaps more than anything else, those people who have an opportunity to invest a bit of themselves in making the decision (through discussion, debate, or whatever) will more than likely support that decision. At least they will not openly oppose it. In short, the greater the openness among the membership in the decision making process, the higher the quality of decision. We repeat: people will support what they help to create.

And that's not all. **Organizations need skillful direction in**

order to produce quality discussions. That is what "Problem-Solving and Decision-Making" is all about. If used as a guideline in solving your problems, you can create a proper perspective and atmosphere among your members that will be conducive to making quality decisions. As a result, the barriers which confront you will become less ominous, and less overwhelming.

Finally, **quality decisions require time.** If all your decisions seem to be the kind that should have been made yesterday, time could well be the problem—a waste of it. Many organizational problems develop as a result of poor planning and just plain old procrastination. Organizational leaders must begin to reach out and anticipate the unforeseen crises and the unknown factors that influence their purposes, goals and objectives. It's not very productive to spend the majority of your time simply reacting to the world around you. You **can** be in control if you anticipate what may be lurking 'round the bend.

Quality decision making and problem solving does require an atmosphere of openness, a sense of direction, and time. It also requires dedication on the part of the entire membership. Leadership **is** everybody's business . . . and so (by the way) are nominations, elections and transitions—the topics we'll cover in Chapter 9.

EXERCISE 10

"PROBLEM SOLVING TRIAD":
PROCESS LEARNING THROUGH PRACTICE AND FEEDBACK

(1 hour)

How To Use This Exercise: This exercise is designed to help three people become more effective in (a) articulating a problem, (b) helping another person clarify a problem and explore alternative solutions, and (c) giving feedback about the observed behavior of the other two participants. It also enhances interpersonal relations within an organization. (Do *not* call this exercise "role-playing!" It is meant to be genuine.)

Supplies: Paper and pencil / pen for each participant.

The Process:

1. Three people agree to take turns articulating a genuine organization-related problem and to practice the process of designing a plan of action to solve it.
2. Each participant takes two minutes to select a definitive problem.
3. One participant agrees to articulate a selected problem, another agrees to be the listener-helper, and the third agrees to be the observer-feedbacker.
4. Prior to starting, each of these three roles is displayed visually, read and discussed so that everyone understands the expected behavior of each role.
5. Each participant has 15 minutes to articulate a problem, come to a plan of action and receive feedback about the process.
6. When each of the three participants has completed the 15 minutes practice feedback session, the remaining time is spent reviewing what has been learned that can be applied to the organization.

The Presenter (The person with the problem.)

1. Selects a genuine organizational-related problem that is a personal concern to him / her.
2. Articulates and clarifies the problem through interaction with the listener.

The Listener (helper)

1. "Tunes in" to another person's problem . . . *really* listens and *hears.*
2. Paraphrases statements for clarity and understanding.
3. Helps proliferate and analyze the alternatives.
4. Offers relevant facts.

   Helpful Hints
   a. Do not interrupt.
   b. Do not give advice, advocate a particular alternative, or express judgments.
   c. Be sincere, genuine and credible; do not "cop out" by being too agreeable.

    d. Maintain eye contact and an attentive body stance.

    e. Be brief (parsimonious) and make your references personal.

    f. Watch for non-verbal cues.

    g. Do not try too hard to be helpful; the responsibility remains with the person who has the problem.

    h. Maintain a relaxed, low risk, non-threatening atmosphere. Be friendly. Express a sense of humor.

    i. Use words like "help *me* understand" and, "what have you tried so far?"

The Observer

1. Is objective while observing, listening and analyzing the process (verbal and non-verbal).

    Helpful Hints

    a. Watch for non-verbal clues.

    b. Limit feedback to *PROCESS* observations to both the *person* with the problem and the *listener* (i.e., keep out of problem content)

    c. Be specific; avoid generalities.

Forming Triads: It is best to have three strangers in a triad, i.c. people from different organizations or hometowns. This increases the probability of risking creativity in a low risk, non-threatening atmosphere essential to learning through practice.

NOTE: This is just an example, please alter to suit your organization. Please refer to "Step II", page 122.

ORGANIZATIONAL RESOURCE INFORMATION CARD

1. *General Information:*

   Name _____ Phone _____

   Address _____ Family _____

   Occupation _____

2. *Background:*

   Of what organizations have you been a member?
   _____

   What offices or committee chairs have you held?
   _____

   What do you usually do in your spare time?
   _____

3. *Resource Information:*

   We have the following committees. Check off two in which you would be most interested.

   Social _____   Publicity _____

   Finance _____   Alumni _____

   Program _____   Membership _____

   Community Service _____

   What job do you think you can perform best and enjoy most?
   _____

   List any skills you have that may help the organization:
   _____

"Nominations are open"
The chairman declares
And all he gets back
Is a bunch of cold stares.

But if he'd been smarter,
And planned a bit more,
The campaign would be lively
And not such a bore.

CHAPTER 9

Nominations, Elections, and Transitions

The granting of power, or delegation of authority within an organization is done by the membership through the processes of nomination and election. The continuity of leadership and direction of an organization is accomplished through various methods of overlapping terms and exchanges of information. In some organizations, continuity and direction includes the collaboration of staff personnel and advisors. Nominating procedures for most organizations are prescribed in the bylaws. Review them and take steps to amend them if they do not include procedures which will insure that the best possible candidates appear on the ballot. Since we are dedicated to the processes most likely to result in the very best results, let's look at some common election practices, and at some alternative methods of nomination, election and transition.

Nominations

With the possible exception of the election itself, the process of nominating officers is the most important step the members will make in determining the quality of leadership for the year ahead. For even if the election runs perfectly and the voter turnout is high, the results will be less than the best if the names of the most qualified members do not appear on the ballot.

Self-nomination is usually done by petition or simply by volunteering. In either case, you **can** infer two things: members who nominate themselves are interested in serving others, and they consider themselves qualified for the position. Either or both may or may not, in fact, be true. Some seem to have their needs met when their names appear on the ballot or when they get elected; they seek ego-satisfaction and are not necessarily qualified. To them, service in office is irrelevant. And the self-perception of being qualified is probably not **entirely** objective. Sometimes it **is** possible to get highly qualified, devoted people on the ballot through self-nomination . . . but don't count on it.

And what about those people who seek re-election, sometimes year after year? Many people will presume that it's just because "no one else wants the job" or "Wanda is just too good to replace." But if leadership **is** everybody's business and if everybody really gets involved, this isn't likely to happen. Remember that by the second time around some officers may have lost some of their spontaneity or zest for trying something new.

Nomination by others is commonly done from the floor or by a nominating committee. Many believe that floor nominations are desirable because they come from the grass-roots of the organization. That is, everybody can get in the act and everybody is eligible for every office. Actually, a nominating committee is an equally democratic way of selecting candidates, providing that committee members are chosen by a democratic process.

Floor Nomination can and often does bring forth qualified candidates, and eliminates those who **aren't** qualified or lack time or interest.

Mr. Walters: "I nominate Trudy Beck for Vice President of International Affairs."

Ms. Beck: "I decline the nomination. I'm afraid I won't be able to attend all the meetings this year, and besides, I don't know anything about international affairs."

But very often nominations from the floor will include a great deal of pressure from peers to accept a nomination, and can include the "blurting" of names with little thought about the candidates' interests, qualifications or availability (as in the example above). It frequently produces **numerous** "I decline the nomination" responses which do nothing at all for the group's image or morale of those present. Still, if floor nominations are required in your bylaws, here are two effective techniques that will improve the quality of the process:

1. State the qualifications and responsibilities of each office orally, or better yet, visually through printed handouts, chalkboards, flip charts or visual projection. Of course, this should be done prior to opening the floor to nominations. This insures more serious and complete consideration of nominees.

2. Organize the membership into small groups of five to eight to discuss various possible nominees and their qualifications. Those most qualified should be questioned by a member of each small group about their interest in serving as an officer and their willingness to devote adequate time to the responsibilities of that office. Nominations can then be made by a representative of the group. This gets everyone involved and eliminates "blurting."

   All nominations are "closed" by a motion which is seconded and passed by a two-thirds vote or by the membership's acceptance of the report of the nominating committee.

Nominating Committees can be either appointed or elected. But be aware that appointed committees, when named by the chair or executive committee, or when these committees include the president or members of the executive committee, are **not** democratic. They tend to perpetuate the point of view of those in office and should be avoided.

Nominating committees can be elected by either of the two methods just discussed: nominating ballot or floor nominations. Small-group interaction gives everyone an opportunity to participate in the decision and, thus, the committee that is selected will be more satisfied with the elected committee process. There will be fewer nomiations from the floor following the report of **this** nominating committee than following the report of one that is appointed.

Members who agree to serve on this committee are also eligible for nomination themselves if it is decided by the committee that one of its own members is the most qualified person available.

The real beauty of nominating committees is that they have the opportunity to study the overall structure of the organization and to match abilities and interests of the membership with the needs of the organization. Still, it is the responsibility of the chair or executive committee to tell the committee members what is expected of them: what offices are to be filled, what qualifications are necessary, how many candidates are needed for each, the amount of commitment required of those nominated, when to report and how to report (whether written or oral).

Some organizations find it useful to obtain an "interest inventory" from each member, either when they join, once a year or as needed (such as by a nominating committee), to determine who is willing to accept responsibility, and what past experiences they've had that are relevant.

We've included an example of such an inventory, (See Exercise 9, Chapter 3) as well as the following nominating committee questionnaire that more specifically defines areas of interest prior to an election.

NOTE: There is no "standard questionnaire. You should design one that best fits the needs of your organization.

NOMINATING COMMITTEE QUESTIONNAIRE

(Note: Return to P. O. Box 846 before November 1st and telephone 916-1776 if you have any questions.)

At the next regular meeting of the Cedar Grove P.T.A. your nominating committee will present to the membership the best possible ballot of people who are seriously interested in carrying out the goals of our organization: to provide the best possible education for our children.

Please check the appropriate boxes to indicate the areas of your greatest interest and your willingness to accept responsibility.

☐ PRESIDENT

☐ VICE PRESIDENT

☐ SECRETARY

☐ TREASURER AND CHAIRPERSON OF THE BUDGET COMMITTEE

☐ NEWSLETTER EDITOR

☐ MEMBERSHIP COMMITTEE

☐ REFRESHMENTS COMMITTEE

☐ FUND-RAISING COMMITTEE

☐ SPECIAL SHORT-TERM PROJECTS COMMITTEE

☐ CALL ME WHEN YOU NEED ME ON A COMMITTEE

My primary concern about our school is:
_____

I feel I can be most helpful by:
_____

PRINT: Name: _____ Phone: _____

Address: _____

_____

Getting Acquainted with the Candidates

When the most qualified candidates have been nominated, the next objective is to acquaint the members with the qualifications of the nominees. Electing the wrong person to an office is a difficult thing to undo. The more direct and personal the getting-acquainted procedure is, the better your election will turn out. Here are two suggesions:

1. Have candidates participate in a symposium-forum with all those running for office "on stage" at the same time. Follow this with questions from an impartial panel of observers and/or from small groups from the membership.

2. Have candidates stand up one at a time in a meeting and give speeches (be sure to set a time limit), then allow time for them to interact with the members in small groups for a limited amount of time. This takes longer, but it is more personal.

The Election

There are many ways to take a vote: voice vote, hand/standing vote or secret ballot.

- **The secret ballot** is the most valid voting procedure since it eliminates the possibility of peer pressure. If you have arranged the membership in small groups to interact personally with the candidates for each office, the balloting can be done office by office while impressions are still vivid in the voters' minds. A representative of each group brings the ballots forward for counting.

- **A hand or voice vote** is used by some very informal organizations to elect candidates office-by-office immediately after nominations from the floor, so that those defeated for one office can be nominated for the next office, and so on. This procedure has little merit except that perhaps in the end every office will be filled. This procedure is based on the assumption that one office is about the same as another, and it only proves that even the most incompetent person can be elected to **something** as long as he or she "just hangs in there" and there are enough offices to go around. Such a practice offers little promise for an outstanding year for the organization and it doesn't do much for the person who is defeated for one office after the other, either. This procedure encourages abuse by popularity votes, honors for other achievements not related to the function of the office, or sidetracking individuals by manipulating them into unwanted posts.

The Transition

The transition between officers at the end of the year is another critical period in the life of an organization. Some organizations, of course, have installation ceremonies involving various combinations of officials and levels of formality, but we are concerned here with going **beyond** formal traditions and courtesies. We want to help the new officers become functionally effective in a new role.

Picture this typical scene: Sally, the newly-elected newsletter editor, approaches Tom, the editor who is leaving office, saying "Gee, Tom, I hope you can help me get started, I've never done anything like this before!"

"Don't worry about a thing, Sally, I've got four boxes of stuff for you."

"Yes, but . . . "

"I'll drop them off at your apartment on my way out of town."

"You're leaving town?"

"Yep! Got a great job up in Manitowok."

"But I've never edited a newsletter and I thought you'd . . . "

"It's simple, I'll write you a letter about it."

"Yes, but . . . "

" 'Bye, Sally—hope to see you again sometime."

The seriousness of this shift of authority varies a great deal from one organization to another. Three practices are common:

- **The "Inside Shuffle."** This is basically an exchange of records and paraphernalia done individually between the old and new officers at the convenience of each pair or at the end of the last meeting. In addition to the exchange of materials, it often includes discussion and note-taking about helpful ideas, procedures and recommendations, as well as traditions, continuing projects and concerns. This can be done briefly and without much interaction or it can be done with some degree of thoroughness. One of the problems with this method is that no one else really knows how thoroughly it was done or if it was done at all. It also denies the other officers the opportunity to understand each others' roles and to start building a team.

Here's a typical scene, this time between two secretaries, Jean and Dale (all other officers are observing):

"Here's a copy of the bylaws, Jean, some important correspondence, and a complete set of the minutes. I think you'll find everything you need here."

"Thanks, Dale, now I guess I'm ready to go to work."

Chris (the new president) interrupts, "Hey, Dale, what about unfinished business from the last couple of meetings? Is that all spelled out in the minutes?"

Dale replies, "Oh, yeah. I'm sure its all in there somewhere."

"Let's postpone discussion of this," suggests Ronny (the outgoing president), "until later when I'll be giving you my stuff, Chris. I have a whole list of unfinished business and suggestions."

Chris: "OK."

Jean continues, "By the way, Dale, I do need to know where to get stamps and supplies, and where the old records are kept. Can we talk about that?"

- **The Special Meeting.** All old and new officers might get together so that everybody can participate in the transition. Not only can the officers pair up to transfer materials and ideas, but there will probably be interaction among all new and old officers. This is an especially valuable experience for new officers . . . it gives them a chance to get to know one another and helps develop an understanding of each officers' aspirations, and organizational roles . . . all important steps toward team-building.

- **The Workshop.** One or more days of working together provides even greater hope for a successful year. A competent consultant can be helpful in making the workshop most effective, especially in team building and goal setting. Some organizations employ staff personnel to carry out various necessary functions and they should always be included in the overall plan of the workshop.

  There are five phases to a complete transition workshop:

1. The first phase features the outgoing officers and a review of the year just past. All outgoing and new officers should be present; each outgoing officer in turn relinquishing records and paraphernalia and giving suggestions that will help the new officer have a successful year.

   Jo: "One thing is for sure, this organization is going to put those environmental freaks in their place this year. I say let's agree on that right now!"

   Chris: "Now wait a minute, Jo, let's not be too hasty. If we expect to get total support from our membership of over 200 people, we'd better not start out the year making big decisions for them."

   Dale: "I agree with Chris. Let's ask our program committee to come up with a series of programs dealing with this whole question of growth and development and its affect on the environment."

   Chris: "I'm not certain that it would be in the best interest of our club to take a definite stand on **anything** political or controversial."

   Jo: "I disagree, but I'll go along with Dale and see what the program committee can come up with."

   When each pair is finished and everyone is satisfied that the new officers are fully equipped to move ahead on their own, the old officers should **leave** the workshop.

2. The second phase is for new officers only and it features team-building. The officers may want to try this on their own but a consultant or staff adviser can make this much more meaningful and productive. Officers alone would be like actors in a play without a director. The consultant can take the group through various exercises

designed to get them to know and appreciate one another as people, bringing about the realization that each person has both hope and talent to offer the team (See Chapter 3, Exercises 2-9.)

3. The third phase involves reviewing the bylaws and the key issues of the year just past as conveyed to the new officers during phase one. For some organizations this may be important and intricate enough to require a period of time to discuss the bylaws and to sift through recent activities to identify those worthy of continuation. Too often, new officers are prone to start the new year with a clean slate as if the organization had no history or prior commitments at all.

4. Phase four involves goal setting (See Chapter 7). A word of caution is appropriate here. The setting of **specific** goals and objectives by a small group of officers without the involvement of the membership may set the stage for membership apathy, for a year of hard work for the officers, and for all the other consequences of establishing an authoritarian relationship between officers and members. Read about Tommy Tyrant in Chapter 12. A more appropriate process during this phase of the workshop is to identify general areas of emphasis for the year ahead. When these broad goals are agreed upon, they should be tentative and subject to the involvement of the membership and in keeping with their absolute and appropriate right of adoption, amendment or rejection.

5. Phase five brings the officers together with others who can be helpful in conducting business and achieving goals. This might include such people as the organization's staff personnel, advisors and alumni—all the outside "experts" that might be of help to the group during the year ahead.

The officers are the people who keep the organization on track and moving toward goals selected through the total involvement of the members. Getting the most qualified, interested and available people nominated and elected is a critical link in the life of an organization. Providing for a thorough transition between sets of officers is like passing the baton in a team relay race. It must be done thoroughly, with everybody participating, and in the presence of a coach if the team (organization) expects to set a good record during the laps ahead.

How are we doing?
We all want to know;
Where have we come from?
And where do we go?

The only true answer
Is sure to be found
Through real introspection,
Not spinning around.

CHAPTER 10

Improvement Through Evaluation

How am I doing? How are we doing? Every successful leader and organization will ask these questions and will seek the answers in a variety of ways and for a variety of reasons. The following examples, however, will give you an idea of the entire process of evaluation, as it is undertaken in far too many organizations:

"Betty, how do you feel the meeting went tonight?"

"I think you did just great, Geraldine, just great!"

"Well, I hope so." (End of evaluation.)

"We're half way through the year, Melvin, and I think we're doing o.k. What do you think?"

"Well, we've lost a few members and attendance is down, but I think you're having a great year, Henry, a great year!" (End of evaluation.)

Improving on this kind of evaluation is what this chapter is all about.

A serious evaluation is a search to find out how you are doing in achieving your goals and objectives. And you should especially want to know how you are doing in the terms of membership satisfaction.

Membership satisfaction should be your first consideration, since it is unlikely that any volunteer organization will survive for long if it believes that **the goal** is more important than **the people** involved in setting and working on the achievement of these goals. It is also unrealistic to expect high levels of goal-achievement without first having a plan for getting feedback from members on how they feel about what's going on.

Evaluating a Meeting

Membership satisfaction (or the lack of it) can be evaluated at any time. During a meeting a sensitive president will pick up cues continuously . . .

When you observe this:	You can infer this:
Philip is yawning, Sandy is gazing out the window, and Clara has no expression on her face at all.	They are uninvolved and probably bored stiff.
The skin on Becky's forehead wrinkles and Norman shakes his head quizzically.	They don't understand what you've said; they don't know what's going on.
Virginia shakes her head with a scowl. Waldo looks at you sternly, and Herman mumbles quietly.	They disagree with you or they may not like what's just been said.
Irene squirms uneasily in her chair, looks at you, looks out the window, shifts her feet, looks at the ceiling, leans forward as if to talk.	Irene is frustrated; she may want to speak, to go home, or go potty.

Leonard grumbles something under his breath loud enough for people around him to hear, and Martha shakes her head angrily.	There is dissatisfaction and perhaps a little hostility in the air.
Julie throws up her hands in futility, John closes his book loudly and looks out the window and Ivan stands up and says "I don't like what's going on here!"	These members are disgusted!

Time after time (when asked) members will say, "I like a meeting when . . .

- I can hear and see and understand what's going on."
- I can get my two cents worth in (and people listen to me)."
- the officers know who I am."
- I feel like we're making progress."
- things aren't railroaded through."
- we don't waste time."

It behooves **you**, then, to do everything possible to respond to these common concerns of members whenever you become aware that something is wrong. It isn't likely that a president of even a relatively small organization can be continuously aware of how every member is feeling about how things are going, but it's important to try.

Face-to-Face Evaluation

One approach to evaluating the feelings of members is to ask them verbally, face to face, what they think. This can be done in a meeting of 15 - 20 members in just a few minutes by asking them, one by one, "How are we doing so far?" "Are the meetings okay?" "What would you like to see changed?"

This can also be done in meetings as large as 100 - 150. The buzz-group process is a very effective way to get some direct feedback on how things are going, personally, for the members. (See Chapter 5, **Using Buzz Groups**.) Members should not expect you to respond to the feedback immediately unless there is some compelling reason for doing so. It might be difficult for you to handle the variety of things being said without being defensive, and in most cases the members probably would not want to extend the length of the meeting for this purpose anyway. The important thing is to make sure that each of them has the opportunity to say their "two cents worth" and it's important for you to listen. Suggestions given by the members as a result of this process should be reviewed and either discussed or acknowledged at the next meeting.

Using a Checklist for Evaluation

A checklist can be used to get as much detailed feedback as you want. On pages 156 and 157 is a list with a four-point rating scale and list of 40 statements, which can be revised, shortened or lengthened to meet your particular needs.

Suggestion boxes can also be used to elicit concerns and get suggestions from members, but unless the notes are signed, there is no opportunity for personal interaction. It does, however, offer a way for members to make an input and perhaps they will feel better about having done so.

General Evaluation

Occasionally, it may be appropriate to ask the members to give feedback that covers more than just a single meeting. On page 155 is a sample of a written questionnaire that can tell you something about how they personally evaluate the way things are going.

Whenever members participate in a survey such as this one, they should, of course, be given feedback themselves. What sorts of changes were indicated in the results of the survey and what is being done about them?

A REQUEST FROM YOUR PRESIDENT

It is important to me that every member enjoy a sense of satisfaction in belonging to and participating in the activities of the Slippery Rock Fine Arts Association. I hope you will take a few minutes to give me your answers to a few questions. You need not sign it unless you want to. A stamped, self-addressed envelope is included for your convenience. May I have it within the next couple of days? Thank you very much.

Charlie Brown

---

1. What do you hope to gain from your membership?

2. What is the most satisfying thing that has happened to you since you joined?

3. What has been your greatest disappointment?

4. What would you like to see changed?

5. Please check the column that most closely reflects your feelings:

	Strongly Agree	Agree	Uncertain	Disagree	Strongly Disagree
Members are given ample opportunity to have their say about every decision.					
The meetings are too informal. We need more parliamentary procedure.					
More concerns of the Association should be referred to committees.					
We should spend more time socially to get to know one another better.					

MEETING EVALUATION FORM

	Poor	O.K.	Good	Great
The Meeting Was Well-Planned				
1. Members were notified in advance	___	___	___	___
2. The notice included main items of business	___	___	___	___
3. There was a pre-arranged agenda	___	___	___	___
4. Officers and committees were ready to report	___	___	___	___
5. The meeting room was pre-arranged	___	___	___	___
The Meeting Was Well-Organized				
6. The meeting started on time	___	___	___	___
7. Guests were introduced and welcomed	___	___	___	___
8. The purposes for the meeting were made clear	___	___	___	___
9. There was a transition from the last meeting	___	___	___	___
10. The agenda was visible for all to see	___	___	___	___
11. One topic was discussed at a time	___	___	___	___
12. One person had the floor at a time.	___	___	___	___
13. Members confined contributions to relevant matters	___	___	___	___
14. The chairman summarized main parts of discussion	___	___	___	___
15. There was correct parliamentary action when needed	___	___	___	___
16. Good use of audio-visual aids were made	___	___	___	___
17. The meeting was moved along at a challenging pace	___	___	___	___
18. Committee assignments were complete and clear	___	___	___	___
19. Plans for the next meeting were announced	___	___	___	___
20. The meeting was adjourned with good timing	___	___	___	___

	Poor	O.K.	Good	Great

The Meeting Had Good Participation

21. Members participated in discussion and voting. . . . .

22. Members participated in planning the agenda. . . . .

23. Members gave suggestions to committees on methods. . . . . . .

24. Responsibilities were widely distributed. . . . .

25. The chairman made good use of questions. . . . .

26. The "pro" and "con" of all issues were considered. . . . .

The Meeting Was Valuable

27. Progress was made toward goals.

28. Something was learned. . . . .

The Program Was Well Done

29. Introductions and responses were well done. . . . .

30. The members were interested and attentive. . . . .

31. The timing was just right (not too short / too long). . . . .

Good Feelings Prevailed

32. Attendance was good. . . . .

33. Everyone was present on time (officers were early). . . . .

34. The members knew one another. .

35. There was some humor during the meeting. . . . .

36. Members and officers helped one another when needed. . . . .

37. There was an atmosphere of free expression. . . . .

38. There was a "warm up" period before the meeting. . . . .

39. Volunteers for committee appointments came quickly. . . . . . .

40. There was evidence of group unity on group goals. . . . .

Evaluating Goals and Objectives

How are you doing with goals and objectives? Organizational **goals** are commonly defined as **general** statements of intent. They indicate particular areas of endeavor to which the organization is committed. They give the organization direction in developing **objectives** which are **specific**, measurable statements of intent.

A goal might read, "to extend the appreciation of the fine arts throughout the community." An objective, within this goal, could read, "to present an arts and crafts show in Slippery Rock Plaza during the month of June with at least 20 exhibitors and 5,000 people attending."

The evaluation of goals raises questions about the **total** performance of the organization. It is the assessment of how thoroughly you are creating programs and events (objectives) by which to achieve organizational goals. It is a general assessment. "What have we done?" "What are we doing?"

The evaluation of an objective, on the other hand, is concerned with the plan of action itself, the nitty gritties. Although the two are inseparable, "goal concerns" pertain to the organization itself whereas "objectives evaluation" refers to questions about how effective and how efficient you were in carrying out a **particular** project.

An Example of Goal Evaluation

Let's say you are evaluating the **goals** of a local school or neighborhood P.T.S.A. (Parent-Teacher-Student Associatioin). The goals of a local PTSA organization might include the following:

1. To enrich the lives of children and youth through music, art, drama and recreation.
2. To expand the involvement and understanding of children and youth in their local environment.
3. To develop understanding of the school's curricular and instructional objectives.
4. To develop an attitude of "our" among all students, parents and teachers.

5. To develop understanding of the school's problems: financial, equipment, discipline, etc., and a cooperative means of solving such problems.

An evaluation of goals would include a general listing of events, activities and projects that were held during the year which would fit under each goal statement. For example:

"GOAL: To enrich the lives of children and youth through music, art, drama and recreation

ACCOMPLISHMENTS DURING THE YEAR

1. Conducted a survey of each student's access to various forms of music, art, drama and recreation, at school, at home and in the neighborhood.
2. Completed a talent survey throughout the neighborhood of people who have knowledge, experience and skills in music, art, drama and recreation.
3. Sponsored Saturday enrichment classes for children in music and dramatics.
4. Informed parents periodically of good TV programs and movies for children."

The vitality of an organization is not measured in the writing of goals (although it is essential to do that) but rather in the activities that are undertaken to accomplish each goal. And remember, the degree of participation and support for each goal and the details of getting it done is directly proportional to the involvement of the membership (in the above case: students, parents and teachers) in setting the goals and developing plans of action. (See Chapter 7.)

An Example of Objective Evaluation

As stated earlier, objectives are more specific than goals. Let's look at a specific event and its evaluation . . .

You were the chairperson of the annual awards banquet which is now over and you have decided to evaluate how well it went. Your banquet objective looked like this:

"There shall be a five-dollar-per-plate, break-even banquet on December 10 to present awards to the three most outstanding new members of the year. The awards will be donated by the alumni, there will be a guest speaker on 'the meaning of volunteerism in a democratic society,' and one hundred members, alumni and guests will be present."

Your evaluation concern is "How effective were we in realizing our objective?" "How close did we come to the target?"

First, analyze the total event and divide it into its various parts. These are the criteria of evaluation. Then establish a means of measuring the degree of perfection.

The format of the evaluation might look something like the sample on page 161.

Member Evaluation?

You have probably noticed by now that we haven't included a form for the evaluation of members by leaders (the "management" point of view). This intentional omission is because our focus is on how organizations can meet the needs of their members, not on how well the members "measure up" to the arbitrary standards of leaders.

We do recognize, however, that from time to time members will want to know "How am I doing?" If the questioner has been actively involved in planning or producing successful programs, you can honestly respond, "Just fine," and no structured evaluation form is needed. If the member is **not** fully participating or seems to be disenchanted with group goals or processes, the situation calls for a different response. Individual criticism won't help, and may hurt, in such circumstances. We believe that the organizational function of leaders is to find out **why** people aren't enthusiastic—through evaluation and by listening (carefully) to unhappy members. In short, by fostering full communication.

Self-Evaluation?

From time to time in the past we have used materials that

AWARDS BANQUET EVALUATION

Criteria	Degree of Perfection			
	Poor	*Good*	*Excellent*	*Perfect*
1. The banquet was held on December 10	___	___	___	___
2. The cost per plate was $5.00 or less	___	___	___	___
3. The banquet broke even financially	___	___	___	___
4. The food was	___	___	___	___
5. Three new members received awards	___	___	___	___
6. They were the most outstanding members	___	___	___	___
7. Awards were donated by alumni	___	___	___	___
8. The guest speaker was	___	___	___	___
9. The guest speaker spoke on the topic	___	___	___	___
10. The guest speaker was properly introduced	___	___	___	___
11. The guest speaker was properly hosted	___	___	___	___
12. There were 100 members, alumni, and guests present	___	___	___	___
13. The service was	___	___	___	___
14. The master of ceremonies was	___	___	___	___
15. Committee members performance was	___	___	___	___
16. The program was	___	___	___	___

Comments and suggestions for next year:

_____

_____

allow members to locate themselves on a "leadership grid" in terms of their personal style. Other materials attempt to help people define their own "personality type." Because such materials are necessarily extremely general and vague, without reference to specific situations or particular organizations, they may be of little immediate or long-term value. We have found them unsatisfactory and sometimes risky to apply.

If you are still concerned about how you may be coming across to others, we suggest a careful reading of Chapter 12 "**Your** Effect on the Group" with attention on how the various leadership styles described can apply to you. You might also seek feedback informally from other group members, keeping in mind that unless you know the person you are asking fairly well, the responses you receive may not be entirely candid or objective.

Very often organizations simply can't fulfill every member's need for thorough feedback on a regular basis. If you need more feedback than your organization can give, don't hesitate to turn elsewhere. Remember, self-knowledge and understanding is a worthy goal but perhaps not one of the primary concerns of your organization. For in-depth assistance you may also need to consider participating in group or individual counseling.

Self-evaluation is often left out of references to the old cliche that "practice makes perfect." The trouble with this trite expression is that you're likely to just get better at doing something worthless, unless you evaluate what it is you are doing. There may be no perfect meeting or event, but thoughtful evaluation, with an appropriate process and the right people, will create the feedback that makes improvement possible.

PART III

Introduction:

Leadership Is . . . Learning More About Yourself, Others, and Group Dynamics

Those of you who are still with us are the people we really want to reach with the information contained in Part III: our guess is that if you've gotten this far and still want more, you **must** be among those who care most deeply about volunteer organizations and the well-being of the people in them.

As we said earlier, the contents of this section are much like the icing on the cake: they are not the **basic** ingredients of good leadership, but include some more sophisticated concepts that will make organizational life a little sweeter and more interesting.

You may find that this is the most creative part of the entire book. Each chapter is the product of many enjoyable hours of conceptual thinking, brainstorming and constructive disagreement about some of the more complex dynamics of organizational behavior. We don't pretend to have all the answers (by any means), and we know that more research is under way on some of these topics. This is a "practitioner's view" of organizational dynamics—things we've come to believe in as a result of our combined 30 years of work with a wide variety of volunteer organizations.

Here's what Part III is all about:

"The Cycle of Organizational Involvement" is a flow-chart interpretation of the cyclical nature of an individual's involvement with a particular group. It is our contention that there are five distinct phases of this process: five points at which an individual makes decisions about the direction and degree of his or her involvement. In **Chapter 11**, we will discuss each of these phases in some detail, as well as suggest how this cycle relates to organizational dynamics.

Chapter 12 concentrates on how **your** personal style as a leader or member of an organization affects the behavior of others in the group. To a great extent, the interaction of these styles can determine the quality of organizational experiences and the amount of satisfaction the members derive from their affiliation with the group. If you're interested in the interpersonal, cause-and-effect relationships of group life, this chapter is especially for you.

We firmly believe that role conflict underlies many of the nebulous (and therefore hard-to-deal-with) aspects of group interactions. Role conflicts arise when one person in an organization has a definite conception of what he or she is supposed to be doing and other members have a different expectation of what the role is all about. In **Chapter 13** we'll explore the realities of such conflicts, and offer some suggestions about how to make things better.

Chapter 14 is about communication: formal and informal, verbal and non-verbal. Communication affects every aspect of group life (meetings, problem-solving, goal-setting, morale, etc.) and is certainly worthy of a deeper examination. You'll find some fundamental explanations of the basic dynamics of communication as well as some games you can use within your organization to improve communication among members and officers. In a way, we've saved this extremely practical chapter as a special reward for the "red hots" in our audience; the concepts and exercises herein should be very helpful to you in a wide variety of group settings.

And finally we have some comments that readers could use for further evaluation and as a guide to getting back to meaningful points in the text for important review.

There's nothing like a circle
To get back to where you've been
When happenings along the way
say "do it all again."

CHAPTER 11

The Cycle of Organizational Involvement

No matter what the goals, activities or policies of your organization may be, most of your concerns as a leader are probably related to what's going on within the membership.

In this chapter we'll attempt to explain a specific set of dynamics that have to do with what we believe to be five basic phases that an individual passes through as a result of getting involved in the life of a particular organization. Along the way, we'll offer some real-life examples of behaviors that are characteristic of each phase, and suggest ways that a leader might enable his or her organization to be more successful in promoting positive feelings among the members.

THE CYCLE OF ORGANIZATIONAL INVOLVEMENT
A FLOW CHART

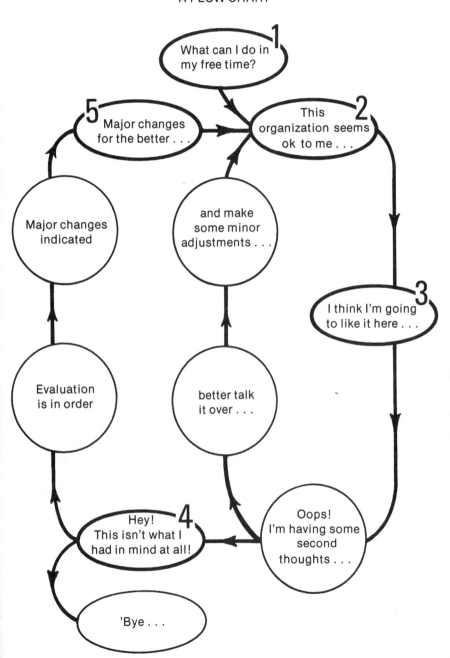

The Five Phases of the Cycle

Phase 1: What can I do with my free time?

Before people can begin to consider joining a group, they must first "take stock" of their real interests, needs and values. These will provide the basis for choosing a group: hopefully, they will be able to find a match between their personal likes, dislikes and aspirations and those of an already-established organization. (See Chapter 1 for more details about how you might accomplish this to help yourself and others.)

Secondly, people must discover what's "out there," and what groups exist; the environment is a vast resource for people in the process of making the decision to get involved with others. This process of learning more about self and the environment is the first phase of The Cycle of Organizational Involvement.

Phase 2: This organization seems O.K. to me...

Organizations have different reasons for wanting to attract new members and for setting particular membership goals. Means of membership recruitment vary too, as do new-member orientation programs and expectations. Individuals also differ in their reasons for seeking group involvement and, in addition, their needs may change from time to time. If the activities of the organization fail to meet the original needs of the member or if the organization doesn't change its programs or policies to meet changing member needs, joiners are likely to become disenchanted, frustrated or unfulfilled. If this happens, they'll either drop out or (if you're lucky) they may take steps to bring about organizational change.

Although it ·is usually implied rather than explicit, membership in volunteer organizations is based on an unwritten "contract" between the person who joins and the organization. That is, a new member expects certain things of the organization, and the organization expects certain things of him or her. The potential member anticipates that some of his or her needs will be met by belonging to this particular organization. For instance, Mary is interested in improving her social status,

Fred wants to meet people and expand his circle of friends, Jack's desire is to serve the community, Jeff has a need to grow personally, Rod is into recreation, and Suzanne wants to increase her income. These people will all be inclined to offer themselves in membership to organizations that will help them achieve these personal goals. If the group also believes that Rod, Mary or Jeff will be helpful in achieving the organization's goals, the membership contract can be confirmed, usually by a "rite of passage" as described earlier.

Phase 3: I think I'm going to like it here...

During this phase, new members attend meetings, participate in discussions, and work on committees and projects. They make new friends and enjoy the activities of the organization. The organization functions well and progress is made toward the attainment of the objectives. Membership is meaningful. This plateau may last a very short time or it may last for quite a long time, but it never lasts forever. During this phase of involvement, members feel good because the organization is somehow meeting their needs. This kind of reinforcement may take many forms. Consider the case of Jody, a relatively new member of the Central City Y.W.C.A.

Jody joined the "Y" because she was planning to invest some of her savings in stocks, bonds or mutual funds, and she had heard that the "Y" would be sponsoring an evening class in "Investments." She paid her dues, was given her membership card, signed up for the class, and was delighted with the information she received during the class sessions. She was so impressed that she decided to sign up for the advanced course, which some of her new friends were also going to take. Jody's association with the Y.W.C.A. was meeting her need to learn about the stockmarket, and her attitude of "being pleased" with her involvement with the "Y" is an example of attitudes typical of people in this phase of the cycle.

Phase 4: Hey! This isn't what I had in mind at all!

Member disruption may be internal or external, small or great. The original promise of the organization may have been misunderstood. The needs of the member may have changed, or the member's expectations of the organization may have changed. The disruption may also result from external forces such as social or policy changes. In any event, when major disruptions occur members begin to express concern about the membership relationship or membership "contract:"

"I joined this club to go on outings and to experience the beauty of nature, not to discuss politics."

"They promised me weekly luncheon meetings, and now I'm expected to help with fund-raising drives at night and on weekends!"

"I thought we were organized to help people in need, but all we do is bicker among ourselves about priorities!"

Alert, sensitive leaders will pick up on this individual dissatisfaction by taking note of such things as irregular meeting attendance, a person's lack of involvement in discussions, and lack of enthusiasm about activities and committee work.

If you see these kinds of things happening in your organization, we suggest you try to find out why. Maybe you can help the dissatisfied member develop a plan for change within the organization; or maybe a compromise between that person and the organization is in order.

There's always the possibility that the dissatisfied person will decide to leave the group anyway (no matter what the changes), and you can help with this transition also. At least he or she will know that you cared about them enough to ask and that you tried to be accommodating. The organization can learn a great deal from these experiences, too.

Phase 5: Major changes for the better

At one time or another in the life of most organizations there comes a time when attendance drops sharply and **most** of the members are not participating in discussions or volunteering for committee work and projects. Informal sub-groups may emerge and, in general, the "natives are restless." Something must be done. It is time for massive change either through a carefully conceived self-study of the organization from within or by asking a qualified unbiased consultant to help. At least three alternatives generally are open to the organization at this point.

- You can change the objectives and activities of the organization to be more in line with the changing interests and needs of the membership.
- You can allow the membership to leave. This is what the most disenchanted members will decide to do anyway.
- You can dissolve the organization. This is the swan song of organizations that fail to respond to the changing needs of their members.

If renegotiation with the membership at each of the decision points is relatively successful, the cycle of individual involvement goes on and on. The organizations that thrive for many years are those that take care of dissatisfaction by making minor adjustments in programs, practices and membership policies as frequently as necessary and before reaching levels of general disruption and experiencing the drastic loss of membership, both of which require major changes in objectives or practices.

The concept that a cycle of organizational involvement actually exists is still relatively new to many of us, and admittedly, it demands further study, revision and discussion. We're including it as what we trust you'll accept as a germinal idea. At least being aware of the idea should give you helpful insights into your group's functions and needs. Let us know if you discover and use other concepts of this cycle.

Leadership is people
The achievement of goals
Elections, resources, status and roles.
But more than all others
You'll have to agree
It's helping and listening
And calling us "WE."

CHAPTER 12

Your Effect on the Group

The process of leadership started when the first two humans interacted to make a decision and give direction to their relationship. Since then, thousands of studies have been done and many papers and books have been written about leadership. Little children do it when they "negotiate" over a toy or cookie, and "big people" do it around international conference tables.

Definitions of leadership differ with situations and philosophies. Military leadership with term-contract personnel is a different process than business leadership with owners, managers and employees. And the leadership in an organization of unpaid equals who volunteer to do a task and who can come and go as they please, is different from either. To make it even more complex, within any leadership situation one can observe varying degrees of authoritarian and democratic behavior.

Even though this book has stressed volunteer task-oriented groups, most of what works between officers and members of these groups will also work between management and employees and in many situations with military and government personnel.

Leadership Defined

Leadership is more than just influencing others. It involves the maintenance of the organization, too: keeping your organization together, satisfying individual needs, encouraging self-direction, promoting interdependence, giving the minority a chance to be heard, listening, responding favorably to constructive behavior and preserving harmony.

Leadership in voluntary task-oriented organizations is the effective blending of two basic concerns . . . those related to **GROUP GOALS** and those related to **GROUP MAINTENANCE**.

Definition:

Leadership is the process of influencing

others in making decisions, setting

goals and achieving goals . . .

and,

concurrently, it is the process of

keeping the group voluntarily together.

Although leadership can be observed in an organization as a relationship between two or more people, each with a unique set of attitudes, needs and personal characteristics, there are other important variables that affect the process.

Leadership Styles Will Vary

Organizations differ in structures, purposes, activities, officer roles, and levels of formality. Some organizations, like the City Planning Commission, may conduct meetings "by the book" using formal motions before discussion, while others, like the local council of the Camp Fire Girls try for general consensus with no motions at all. The Cedar City Kiwanis Club may give its committees authority to make decisions, whereas the school board of trustees may require committee reports as recommendations for membership action. Still others may use committees to define a problem, gather facts, identify alternative courses of action and the consequences of each . . . with considerable membership involvement in making the final decision. All of these internal workings of an organization affect the leadership behavior of individuals.

Leadership Styles Are Affected by External Factors

Being "chartered," for example, affects the organizational life of a membership; a chapter of a national fraternity operates from a **different** set of expectations than a "local." The national office provides all sorts of paraphernalia: an emblem, jewelry, stationery, a book on the organization's history and traditions and procedures for conducting meetings and expanding the membership. Field secretaries visit local chapters to help solve local problems and to bond the chapters together under a single national image. The patterns and norms of leadership behavior are made perfectly clear.

A local fraternity, on the other hand, plays it all by ear. There is no orchestration except that which persists as members come and go. Whatever the membership wants to emphasize in any one year is o.k.; and their image might change from one extreme to another and back again without any continuing external influence whatever.

Some Important Leadership Qualities

Much has been written about personal qualities that are necessary for effective leadership, but this approach to explaining the leadership process leads to sterile ground. There is little doubt that it helps to be friendly and have a touch of grace and charisma. But there is no substitute for being sensitive to others and responding competently with a group process that fits the occasion. Nor can we dispute the notion that in order to relate to others effectively you must first relate to yourself. If you don't love and respect yourself, how can others love and respect you? It is essential to effective interpersonal relations that people not only anticipate being treated with love, dignity, and consideration, but that they treat others in the same manner. People in leadership positions should be the **first** to reach out. Openness and consideration **of** others begets consideration of oneself **by** others.

As the president of an organization you must not only develop the ability to assess the membership situation as it continues to change throughout a meeting and throughout the year, but you must have the ability to respond with appropriate group processes. (See Chapter 14.)

You must be competent in using such group processes as brainstorming, role-playing, buzz groups, informal discussion and parliamentary procedure. You must also learn to select the **best** process at the **right time** to meet the present situation. This takes a sense of awareness and timing that is all too rare in organizational life today.

Time and Its Impact on Leadership Styles

Any consideration of leadership behavior would be incomplete without understanding the tremendous influence that the lack of adequate time has on leadership styles. Democratic processes take time. Whenever the lack of time hangs heavy over a decision, the atmosphere necessary for maximum membership involvement becomes stifling. Even when you believe in "open" meetings and the importance of membership involvement and support of decisions, you will find yourself pressed into uncomfortable, "pushy" tactics to get through a long agenda. Give everyone a copy of the agenda, place it on a chalkboard or on newsprint, or project it on a screen for all to see. This will help everybody set the pace of the meeting. Work between meetings to have all agenda items completely ready for membership action. (See Chapters 4 and 6.)

Assertiveness and Leadership

During recent years considerable attention has been given to the analysis of assertive, non-assertive and aggressive behavior, and the effect of such behavior on both self and others. Behavior modification counselors agree that behavior and attitudes are learned throughout life and that behavior which proves to be inappropriate or non-productive can be changed. The non-assertive person can learn to become more assertive and the aggressive person can change behavior style to become more responsive to the needs and values of others.

Alberti and Emmons (1978) have developed a chart contrasting assertive with non-assertive and aggressive actions. It shows that, "in the case of the **non-assertive** response in a given situation, the person is typically denying himself and is inhibited from expressing his or her actual feelings. He often feels hurt and anxious as a result of his inadequate behavior. Allowing others to choose for him, he seldom achieves his own desired goals. The person who carries his desire for self-assertion to the extreme of **aggressive** behavior accomplishes his ends usually at the expense of others. He usually hurts others in the process of making choices for them, and minimizing their worth as persons."

You will find these attitudes and behaviors, and others exemplified a little later in this chapter as we describe five basic leadership styles formed in volunteer organizations.

The Fundamental Relationship: You and Me

The **process** of leadership can be summed up in one very simple relationship: you and the other person. Although a great deal has been written about this basic relationship, there are three interpretations we have found to be particularly pertinent to the topic at hand.

Martin Buber's "I and Thou"

Buber presents this relationship between people delicately and personally in his classic *I and Thou.* [1] The "I" attitude is translated into "**I** am a person and you are an 'it'," whereas the "thou" point of view would say, "I am a person and you are a person."

Douglas McGregor's "X" and "Y" Theory

McGregor develops a similar concept in his "X" and "Y" theory of management. When presented as a grid, the "X" axis represents the degree of direction and control imposed on a person from without, and the "Y" axis the degree of integration and self-control imposed by a person from within. [2]

McGregor's assumptions about these axes are:

"X" Theory	**"Y" Theory**
1. The average human being has inherent dislike of work and will avoid it if he can.	1. When physical needs are satisfied, social needs emerge (belonging, acceptance, friendships and love); these give way to concern about self-esteem and respect by others. Above all, is the need for self-fulfillment; that is realizing your potentialities for self-development and for being creative.

1. Buber, Martin, *I and Thou* (translation, prologue and notes by Walter Kaufmann). New York: Charles Scribner's Sons, 1970. Used with permission.

2. From *The Human Side of Enterprise* by Douglas McGregor. Copyright © 1960 by McGraw-Hill, Inc. Used by permission of McGraw-Hill Book Company.

2. Because of this human characteristic of dislike of work, most people must be coerced, controlled, directed, or threatened with punishment to get them to put forth adequate effort toward the achievement of organizational objectives.

3. The average human being prefers to be directed, wishes to avoid responsibility, has relative little ambition; he wants security above everything.

2. People exercise self-direction toward objectives to which they are committed, this being a function of self-satisfaction associated with achievement.

3. People learn, under favorable conditions, not only to accept responsibility but to seek it. Avoidance of responsibility, lack of ambition, and emphasis on security are generally the results of experience, **not** inherent human characteristics.

4. The capacity to exercise a relatively high degree of imagination, ingenuity, and creativity is widely, **not** narrowly distributed in the population.

Blake and Mouton's Approach

Blake and Mouton (1964) propose the extreme four corners plus the center of a grid as key orientations for achieving industrial production through people. They reject the need to select one theory over another and believe, instead, that there are many possibilities for blending various leadership styles in different management situations.

The grid approach to the relationship between self and others has been adapted to many human situations by Blake and Mouton in several diverse kinds of publications.

Although we have found the managerial grid an excellent device to bring out the extreme four corners of "I and Thou" behavior in volunteer membership organizations, we have developed our own "Five-Style" approach.

Five Basic Styles of Leadership

In a voluntary membership group, the two-dimensional process of influence between people is easily observed. It is simply a matter of the degree of regard and concern you have about yourself and **your** needs versus the degree of regard and concern you have about others and **their** needs.

What follows is a presentation of five basic styles that we believe are fairly typical of organizational leaders. Keep in mind that these are intentional exaggerations, and that no one uses the same style day in and day out. Your degree of concern for self and others changes from situation to situation, and from one group to another.

Tommy Tyrant

Tommy Tyrant's the kind of guy who loves to be in control: of himself, of a meeting, of the resources, of other people. He's the dyed-in-the-wool aggressive leader, and because many of his needs are "me" (and my ego) oriented, he will very often work himself into a position of organizational leadership.

	WHAT DOES TOMMY DO?	HOW DO OTHER MEMBERS RESPOND TO TOMMY?
Style of conducting meetings.	He talks, talks, talks and talks. Of course, other members can talk, too, but *only* with his permission and only *to* Tommy.	They listen, listen, listen, listen. Usually with only half an ear; frequently, they fall asleep.
Room arrangement.	He arranges the meeting room so everyone is facing him. Too much conversation among the members is distracting and *can* be dangerous, as well.	They look toward Tommy (since they don't have much choice), but because that's not much fun, they study the wall behind Tommy, the ceiling above Tommy and the picture beside Tommy, etc.
Attitude about sharing resources and information.	Tommy keeps meeting agendas and program plans to himself. Why should anyone else need to know what's going on?	They wonder about how much longer the meeting's going to last, what's coming up next, where the refreshments are, if there will be any discussion.
Attitude about member participation and fulfillment.	He advocates his own ideas and either criticizes or ignores all others. After all, he has more good ideas than anybody else around . . .	They either accept Tommy's ideas without question (or commitment) or they silently reject Tommy's ideas and resent him.
Decision-making style.	Tommy makes decisions unilaterally or with a small group of cronies. He then simply announces to the group what "their" next project will be.	Some members just disappear. Those who don't, grudgingly work on "Tommy's projects" because of loyalty to the group, fear of rejection or punishment, or hope of reward.

Dora Doormat

Dora Doormat is a **really nice, non-assertive person**: kind, considerate, hard-working and quiet (maybe even a little shy). She wants everybody to be happy, and so to avoid hassles within her organization, she volunteers to do all that "dirty work" that no one else wants to do. She may have found herself in a position of leadership simply because no one else would accept the responsibilities of office—anyway, she smiles a lot . . .

	WHAT DOES DORA DO?	HOW DO OTHER MEMBERS RESPOND TO DORA?
Style of conducting meetings.	She listens, listens, listens, listens . . . agrees, agrees, agrees, agrees. (She nods her head in the affirmative a lot, too.)	They talk, talk, talk and talk, without direction. They soon become frustrated because nothing ever seems to happen.
Room arrangement.	She sets up the room in whatever way the members like it. Rows and columns today, circles next week, pillows on the floor next month . . . whatever.	They like Dora's flexibility and affability at first, but eventually they become disappointed by the lack of progress toward their goals.
Attitude about sharing resources and information.	Her files are an open drawer to anyone who wants access to them. She willingly gives things to people, but seldom gets them back; and frankly, the club records are a mess.	They form splinter groups around self-appointed leaders who promise to "get things back in order." This results in internal competition and a weakening of group unity.
Attitude about member participation and fulfillment.	She is *extremely* concerned about the welfare of others; to the exclusion of consideration of her own needs. She seldom suggests ideas of her own, *never* dominates a conversation, and doesn't stop anyone from having their say.	They *like* Dora because she goes out of her way to make people happy, but they resent her lack of leadership. Too many issues are left unsettled and ambiguous as a result of Dora's need to avoid conflict at any cost.
Decision-making style.	She never makes decisions on her own, and seldom requires her organization to make them. If you don't choose one alternative over another, no one ever loses, and no one ever gets angry.	After a while, just having fun and being happy isn't enough. They lose interest and may either look for a more productive organization or replace Dora as soon as possible.

Betty Backandforth

Betty Backandforth does just that: she goes back and forth between being aggressive and being non-assertive, between over-emphasizing the importance of group production and being **overly** concerned about the emotional needs of the members. Betty is also extremely sensitive to the way people respond to her, and if she picks up vibrations that she's working people too hard one week, she'll cancel the meeting and treat everyone to pizza the next. The **problem** is that no one knows whether she's going to be wearing her salt-mine hard hat or her best party dress from one meeting to the next: she's totally unpredictable and therefore difficult to work with.

	WHAT DOES BETTY DO?	HOW DO OTHER MEMBERS RESPOND TO BETTY?
Style of conducting meetings.	She will use different meeting styles to correspond with what she perceives to be the *mood* of the members. If they seem to feel positively about her, she'll work them hard and proceed *by the book*; if they begin to resent her pushing, she'll halt the proceedings and suggest that they do something fun or social.	They never know whether to dress for pizza or for work. They resent the fact that meetings can be adjourned at a moment's notice, and feel like they're being manipulated into doing what Betty wants them to do, when she wants them to do it. As Betty vacillates between being Tommy Tyrant or Dora Doormat, it's downright confusing.
Room arrangement.	Again, this depends on what kind of vibrations Betty is picking up. If it's a work meeting, it'll be rows and columns; if not, it'll be loose and conducive to interaction.	They get tired of moving things around, and wish Betty would make up her mind
Attitude about sharing resources and information.	Sometimes she'll share and be very open about things; other times she'll demand respect, privacy and submission. You just never know.	They hesitate to approach Betty, for fear that their requests will be ill-timed or inappropriate to her mood. If they ask the wrong question at the wrong time, they'll be in hot water.
Attitude about member participation and fulfillment.	When she's in an "anything you say" frame of mind, the needs, ideas and wishes of the members will come first. If she catches them sloughing off, though, and not accomplishing group goals, she'll come on like gangbusters, and crack down.	They appreciate Betty's commitment to group goals (things *do* get done), and they generally feel that she cares about their personal needs. But why does she have to be so extreme and unpredictable?
Decision-making style.	Because Betty always wants to stay on the winning side, her usual means of solving a problem is to take a vote on it, leave it to chance (flip a coin) or consult an expert. Thus, nobody can blame *her* if something doesn't work out.	They always know some people will "win," but invariably others must "lose." When Betty only has 51% *for* her, 49% are still *against* her. People who have good ideas but no influence in the group usually end up with the short end of the stick, and thus many valuable members just drift away.

Irving Indifferent

Poor Irving's really "had it." If you think of all the apathetic people you've ever known, and then multiply their indifference by 10 . . . well, that's Irving. He honestly didn't **want** to be president for the third year in a row, but there really wasn't anybody else to do it, so Irving hesitantly agreed. He could care less . . . zzzz.

	WHAT DOES IRVING DO?	HOW DO OTHER MEMBERS RESPOND TO IRVING?
Style of conducting meetings.	He's *definitely* disorganized, and hopelessly unprepared. There's no agenda, no program, no refreshments—sometimes there isn't even a *room* when Irving forgets to reserve one.	They're confused and unhappy. They can't understand how Irving got to be president in the first place; who would elect someone who doesn't even care enough to remember to reserve the room?
Room arrangement.	Oh, it doesn't really matter. Whatever's there is O.K. by Irving, just so there's no big hassle about it.	They're spread out all over the place; talking among themselves, playing "Hangman" on the chalkboard, amusing themselves. A newcomer would think the meeting hadn't started yet.
Attitude about sharing resources and information.	What information? What resources? Irving quit filing things two years ago, and the records are God-knows-where. Sure, he'd share things if he could, but there's nothing to be found —*anywhere*.	They don't know what's going on or how to initiate anything. Irving can't help them . . . no one seems to care. What's the history of the organization, anyway? What's been done by members in the past?
Attitude about member participation and fulfillment.	If the members want to go ahead and fulfill themselves, that's perfectly all right with Irving. But he's too preoccupied with other things to be of much help.	They resent Irving's "do nothing" attitude, and wish he'd step aside and let someone else take over. There are some new members who have joined since Irving was elected, and some of them would *like* to hold office.
Decision-making style.	Haphazard, "factless" and almost imperceptible. Irving just doesn't want to bother with making decisions; whatever happens, happens.	They lose interest rapidly and probably stop coming to meetings. Why should they? Irving misses as many as anybody, himself.

Patience Perfect

Patience is an example of what we believe is a perfect leader. Though few of us ever attain this level of assertiveness and perfection in our day-to-day organizational lives, we feel that this style produces the most positive results in terms of member satisfaction, goal achievement and interpersonal affection and respect. Thus, especially when your group must make major decisions, plan significant programs, establish important policies or reach a consensus, we suggest that you use this style, to the best of your ability. (**Consensus** is, literally, "consent to agree." It is used here to define that level of agreement that occurs when everyone in a decision-making group will support the decision **to some** degree. That is to say, no one will actively oppose a consensus decision. It is general agreement and it denotes group solidarity behind the decision.)

	WHAT DOES PATIENCE DO?	HOW DO OTHER MEMBERS RESPOND TO PATIENCE?
Style of conducting meetings.	Her conduct of meetings depends on what needs to be accomplished. When information must be communicated, she's most likely fairly formal, but when decisions must be made or some new ideas are needed, Patience uses interaction or "buzz" groups to involve the membership. The agenda is always prepared well ahead of time, and provides for member input.	They respond well to Patience's behavior. They know that the meetings will be organized and productive, and also that they will have the opportunity to voice their opinions and to participate fully. Mutual trust and respect develop as the foundation for teamwork. Participation is high and members can be spontaneous.
Room arrangement.	She arranges the room to meet specific needs of the group, and so the set-up can change from week to week. Patience makes sure that everyone can see and hear what's going on, she uses as many visual aids as possible, and she sees to it that people are comfortable.	They look forward to meetings because they're not always dull or repetitious. Even though Patience provides for variety, however, the scene is never chaotic or disorganized—only different and interesting. Members can see, hear and respond.
Attitude about sharing resources and information.	Patience isn't afraid of depending on others to accomplish a task or achieve a goal. She spends time with anyone who needs information or assistance and isn't selfish with what she knows. If it can help someone do a better job, its theirs for the asking.	They are willing to volunteer for things because they know they'll get the help and support they need to complete the assignment. By spreading the responsibility widely, Patience brings about greater productivity and team feeling. Work and satisfaction go on even when she's not present. People care!
Attitude about member participation and fulfillment.	In a group of 8, Patience only takes up 1/8 of the "air time," and doesn't hog the floor. Even though she values her opinions and ideas, she knows that others also have much to offer, and so she encourages two-way dialog and honest interaction. Self-fulfillment and other-fulfillment are equally important to her.	They experience personal growth and satisfaction, and have a chance to develop their leadership potential within the organization. Their morale is high and their commitment is strong. They know that minor disagreements can be settled without hostility, and that their opinions will be heard.
Decision-making style.	In a pinch (crisis), Patience may resort to taking a vote or making a decision on her own, but she prefers to take the time to reach a consensus on major issues. She listens to both sides carefully and then lets the members decide.	They feel good about organizational decisions. Nothing is "laid on them" or railroaded through. They will support all that they have created together.

Let us stress again that these styles are **extremes**. In reality, there are countless variations of each of them: people have widely varying degrees of concern for self and concern for others.

Our intention is simply 1) to make you more aware of some combinations of behavior that can have tremendous positive or negative impact on organizational progress and processes, and 2) perhaps to help you identify some behaviors **you** might have that are counter-productive. All of these styles are extremely changeable, evasive and complex: A Tommy Tyrant at the lunchtime Lion's Club meeting may be a Dora Doormat in the presence of his boss and immediate supervisor two hours later.

Why Are There So Many "Tommy Tyrant" Leaders?

One need not look far to find autocratic and aggressive "Tommy-type" leaders in volunteer membership organizations. In fact, the difficult task is to find a single democratic Patience Perfect leader! Why is this? Why is it that so many leaders feel that people must be led, directed and coordinated? Why do they feel that members must be motivated by public praise and awards? Why do they feel it is necessary to control the flow of information to members? Why do so many leaders "keep their distance" from the membership?

Gibb classified authoritarian or paternalistic behavior as DEFENSIVE because dynamically the autocratic leader is defending himself or herself against fears and distrusts and against perceived or anticipated attack from the outside. This authoritarian or defensive view is understandable in the light of certain aspects of the culture we live in:[3]

- A life of vertical hierarchy, prescribed role responsibilities and delegated authority.
- Current dominant values of efficiency, excellence, productivity and task performance.

---

3. Gibb, Jack R., *Dynamics of Leadership,* from the book, *In Search of Leaders.* Editor, G. Terry Smith; Publishers, American Association of Higher Education, 1967.

- The impersonality, alienation, loneliness, impotence and indifference of our people.
- A world of automation, data programming and processing.

Gibb contends that defensive leadership is highly inappropriate and perhaps even fundamentally dissonant with another side of the world we live in:

- Education for growth, intimacy, authenticity, humanness and creativity.
- The Judeo-Christian ethics of love, honesty, intimacy, faith, cheek-turning and brotherhood.
- A climate for research, inquiry, scholarship, contemplation and learning.
- Cooperation, group planning, team building and various successful forms of group effort.
- A world of ambiguity, feeling, conflict, sorrow, creativity and diversity.
- A world of people.

The dynamics of defensive leadership are centered on fear and distrust. Leaders who have varying degrees of fear about their own inadequacy and how they are seen by others tend to do several things:

- They distrust the people being led who are lazy, irresponsible, uninspired and apathetic.
- They filter the information that is given to the followers in order to allay fears, to increase morale and to justify action taken by the leader.
- They induce the acceptance of leadership goals by followers through skilled persuasion.
- They attempt to control and manipulate the motivations and behavior of the followers with new incentives and gimmicks to show leader approval when old ones become ineffective.
- And the incidence and degree of low trust, strategic and controlling behavior of leaders varies directly with the amount of fear.

What To Do About Tommy Tyrants

Although the above is both observable and deplorable throughout all kinds of organizations, it is especially offensive and inappropriate in volunteer membership groups where freedom and spontaneity and the sharing of responsibility is what holds them together.

If defensive, autocratic (Tommy Tyrant) leadership is so inappropriate, especially in volunteer membership groups, what can we do to develop in leaders those behaviors which center on a high degree of trust and confidence in people?

Neither the many things necessary for change, nor the processes for bringing changes about will be easy to prescribe, for we have inherited an overdose of Tommy Tyrant models who have made it to high places of authority and power, even in our democratic society. Patience Perfect leaders with a great deal of self-acceptance and personal security, who are open and freedom-giving, and who place a high value on self-satisfaction and self-respect for everybody, do not seek nor do they receive the kind of public rewards that make them obvious models for others.

Those of us who are aware of or care about the schism between autocratic and humane leadership styles can learn the essential content and processes of participative leadership by our own actions:

- Try experiencing workshops designed to demonstrate the results of total membership interaction and consensus.
- Try practicing selected skills to improve members' ability to communicate with others, such as listening, paraphrasing and questioning.
- Try developing through practice a repertoire of group processes that get all members (including the officers) involved with one another and foster interdependence.
- Try assessing the long-term, beautiful consequences of "Patience Perfect" leadership behavior.
- Try anticipating the future through group imaging, goal setting and plans of action.
- Try being available, opening up, trusting others and giving them a variety of opportunities to share their ideas, make decisions, explore goals and experiment with many different activities.
- Try making easily available to members all information about the organization.

- Try sharing with other leaders the pains of fear, distrust and control and the joy of trust and self-motivated members.

Just try it . . . we think you'll like it!

Our roles are evasive.
As everyone knows
They change with occasions
As often as clothes.

But don't YOU be fooled
By how others appear;
For if you'll look closely,
Their roles will be clear.

CHAPTER 13

Overcoming Role Conflict

A **role** is what a person does or is expected to do in a given situation. It is a set of expectations placed upon a person in a particular position that is based on how others have behaved in that position in the past, and by the limits that are placed on that role in formal membership requirements and officer responsibilities. In a highly-structured organization, the range of acceptable role behavior of an officer or a member may be very narrow. In most informal volunteer membership organizations, however, considerable variation in role behavior is tolerated.

This wider range of permissible role behaviors can give you more freedom to carry out your responsibilities, but it can also open up a "Pandora's box" for all sorts of perceptual role conflicts. Whether these conflicts are minor or major, they are always disruptive of group morale and productivity.

Role conflict becomes an organizational problem when two or more people interpret or perceive the same situation differently, and their interpretations result from different sets of concepts, values and attitudes; or when they attach different sets of expectations to a given role.

The Dynamics of Role Conflict

The Example of Happy Harry. Happy Harry has been elected president of the newly-formed Downtown Improvement Society. Where is Harry coming from? How does he perceive the situation?

"I'm in a position of great status, the central figure in important civic issues, a person with the responsibility to bring about major changes in the appearance of the downtown area, a leader with the authority to make decisions and organize and carry out a plan of action."

Harry's Image of Anticipated Results: "If I do this job right, I'll be selected 'Citizen of the Year'."

Harry's Perception of the Way Others Interpret His Role: "The City Council expects me to get the job done efficiently, and the downtown merchants are busy with their businesses. They just want me to let them know when and how I think the project will affect them. The members of the society want me to exert leadership and tell them what to do and the other officers expect nothing more than to be cogs in the machine that's going to get this show on the road."

Harry's Concepts, Values and Attitudes (How He Perceives Himself and Others): "I always seem to have the best ideas about what needs to be done and how to do it. I believe most people want to avoid responsibility and work even if they **do** join a society like this. But I've dealt with people like this before, and I know how to use a little gentle persuasion to get them to see it my way and do their share of the work."

Where Are the Others Coming From? How do the members and other officers of his committee, the merchants and the City Council perceive the situation?

"The members of this society have always worked together as equals toward the development of an attractive and functional downtown area." . . . "Since the downtown merchants stand to benefit most from this project, we expect to be consulted every step of the way. After all, we **are** the proprietors of what the downtown is all about" . . . "Harry had better work directly with the city planning commission on every detail of the project or there may be no approval from the City Council."

Others' Perceptions of Harry's Role: "He should help us become a team so that we can enjoy this venture; his primary function is to help us get all our ideas and resources out in the open. I want him to be informal and unhurried so we can have the time to get total agreement on everything we decide."

How Does Harry Behave? "This meeting will come to order!" (Gavel bangs twice.) "I know you will all be pleased to know that I have worked out a plan whereby we can all get right into this project. There will be three sub-committees, and I have made the assignments as follows bla . . . bla . . . bla . . . etc. And, I want the chairman of each group bla . . . bla . . . bla . . . etc. Are there any questions? Good! That will be all for tonight. The meeting is adjourned." (Gavel bangs once.)

We have here, folks, a donnybrook-level role conflict. And even though we have purposely given an extreme example of this organizational problem, similar misunderstandings are a common occurrence and are internally disruptive in varying degrees.

What are some common role-conflict situations?
- Conflict between officers and outside authorities such as school, church and fraternal advisors and officers.
- Conflict between elected officers and staff employees of the organizations.
- Conflict between or among officers.
- Conflict between an officer and member.

SETTING THE STAGE FOR ROLE CONFLICT

Preventing Role Conflict

The key to prevention of role conflict is a clear role definition or clarification through effective communication.

If the potential role-conflict situation is related to a new organization with new officers or a continuing organization that is changing officers at the end of the year, take the time and share some experiences that will help people get to know one another, some that will build a sense of team purpose. Include in these experiences appropriate roles for various officers and members. (See Chapter 3, Exercises 2-9.)

If it is a matter of instructing a committee about its responsibilities or delegating authority to a member to carry out a specific task: 1) When you accept a responsibility, be exactly as thorough, as explicit, as inspiring as you would like someone else to be. 2) Take nothing for granted. If you really spell out the task, and ask for explicit feedback, you'll know the job is in capable hands. A good test, if you want to go all the way, is to write down what you think is supposed to happen and ask the other person to write down what he/she thinks is supposed to happen. Then discuss any discrepancies.

How to Identify Role Conflicts and Discrepancies: Two Examples

Example 1: Alice, the president of an Outings Club of 50 members used about 10 minutes of a meeting to get direct feedback from the membership about what her role should be. She came prepared with 10 statements which she read aloud, asking each member to rate his/her level of agreement with each statement.

Rating	Meaning
1	I strongly agree
2	I agree
3	I am undecided
4	I disagree
5	I strongly disagree

The statements she used were: "As president of our club, I should:

1. Start meetings at 7:00 p.m. sharp, regardless of how many people are present.
2. Have most of the decisions made by the executive committee before the meeting and present them for your approval at the meeting.
3. Provide for maximum participation of all members present at meetings in the making of all decisions.
4. Require all decisions be made by parliamentary procedure.
5. Require an oral report of each outing, by the trip leader, at the first meeting after the event.
6. Require an evaluation of each outing, by participants, at the first meeting after the event.
7. Arrange for an entertaining program at each meeting.
8. Arrange for a demonstration of outing skills at each meeting.
9. Keep meetings to no longer than an hour and a half.
10. Devote more time to getting members to know one another better."

It is a simple matter to tally the score on each question and have available an all-member summary of responses to your concerns, for your immediate use, or future study by the executive committee.

The questions, of course, must relate to the basic concerns and purpose of the organization, and the amount of time spent on role clarification should be a reflection of the seriousness of the situation or the potential conflict. For major problems, it is best to get the membership involved in talking it out, in small groups, with consensus-oriented discussions and with provisions for giving constructive feedback to the presiding officer.

Example 2: Betty, the president of the Community Coordinating Council, was required by the bylaws to make several appointments of persons to represent the organization on commissions throughout the community. She had many responsibilities and didn't feel that she had the time to do it herself, so she appointed Steve:

"Steve, will you help me with a little job? I'm really very busy!"

"Sure, what is it?"

"I have to appoint people to 12 different commissions and I need someone to put it all together for me."

"O.K. Don't worry about a thing. I'll have them all lined up for you so that you can sign the letters of appointment before the end of the month."

"Thanks a lot, Steve, I'd sure appreciate that."

Steve was a highly motivated person committed to doing the best possible job. He felt that it was his role to recruit, interview and select the most qualified individuals available, and to prepare letters of appointment for Betty's signature. But Steve became confused, then angry when he learned that Betty was making some appointments on her own without consulting him. He considered resigning but, instead, asked a third party for help. Mediation may have sufficed, but an analysis of the role as it related to and was viewed by both parties resulted in use of the following "Role Clarification Form" with both parties. With the information presented on the completed forms, Betty and Steve were able to see their different perceptions of the role Steve was to play in setting up the commission appointments.

ROLE CLARIFICATION FORM

	Strongly Agree	Agree	Disagree	Strongly Disagree
1. It is Steve's responsibility alone to recruit applicants.				
Explain				
2. The interviewing of people interested in commission work is the responsibility of Steve alone.				
Explain				

	Strongly Agree	Agree	Disagree	Strongly Disagree
3. Steve should have a complete data sheet on the qualifications of each person interviewed.				

Explain _____

| 4. Steve should inform the president of the qualifications of each person interviewed and explain why he is recommending one over the others. | | | | |

Explain _____

| 5. The appointment of a person to a commission is Betty's responsibility as president. | | | | |

Explain _____

| 6. It is appropriate for the president to select someone on her own as long as she tells Steve about it. | | | | |

Explain _____

| 7. Steve should give Betty frequent progress reports including the names of people he is considering. | | | | |

Explain _____

Such an instrument becomes the vehicle through which two individuals with conflicting perceptions of a role can get together and discuss their responses to these five pertinent questions prepared by the consultant, who may or may not be invited to participate in the discussion between the two.

The instrument is simple and the process is simple; use it. It is neither wise nor prudent to allow conflict caused by divergent role perceptions to go unresolved.

Two other concepts that are directly related to role conflict are motivation and communication. **Luckily for you**, these are precisely the focus of the next chapter.

204

If you hope for a lot of successes,
Don't settle for just second guesses.
Make efforts to say
"How's it going today?"
And you'll surely avoid
Future messes.

CHAPTER 14

Understanding Motivation and Communication

Throughout the book, you've probably been looking for some ideas on how to motivate people, and how to be sure that people understand what you say and what you write. We discussed motivation briefly in Chapter 7 and we have shown how to apply the principles of motivation in other chapters. People are motivated when they make a leisure decision and take action to do something (like becoming a member of a group); when they are participating in a discussion or helping to make a decision; when they are setting goals, working on committees, voting in an election or evaluating an activity.

What Makes Peter Run?

Motivation involves energy being spent and it involves the anticipation of something desirable happening as the **result** of energy being spent. It also involves emotion, that is, having feelings about something in the environment that you are aware of. For instance, when Peter attends his first meeting, you know that he spent some energy to get there, and you infer that:

- He is aware that the meeting was being held.
- He expected something to happen which would make him feel good (something that would satisfy his interest or needs).

The process of motivation is the same whether Peter attends a meeting, volunteers to work on a committee, or sits next to an attractive woman. Remember that it is Peter's energy, Peter's awareness and Peter's interests and needs that will or will not cause any of the above actions. About all you can really affect (without knowing Peter personally) is his awareness of the meeting through publicity or an invitation from a member. Peter alone is the master of his energy system's values, and his emotions, and he can turn them on or off whenever his interests and needs come into conscious contact with something in his environment.

Another key factor affecting Peter's motivation requires that he must see the goal he seeks as one that is **attainable**, based on his past experiences of success and failure. If his purpose in attending your meeting is to meet people and to make some new friends, and no one pays any attention to him, he may very well conclude that this goal is not attainable in your club and never return.

The level of Peter's aspirations and his chances of attaining them at these levels are affected by his understanding and knowledge of his past experience. For example, his decision to settle for just meeting people and making some new friends rather than hoping to become an officer, a committee chairman or even a committee member may have been influenced by some earlier experience when he tried for this kind of recognition and failed to achieve it.

As you can see, we believe that many of the factors that influence motivation are beyond the grasp of anyone else, thus suggesting that it might be best to concentrate on those very few ways that you **can** exert influence. When Peter comes to you or attends a meeting where you preside, do what you can:

- Encourage him to talk.
- Listen to him.
- Get others to listen to him.
- Make him aware of the many activities he can choose

from—as an observer or participant—whatever **he** wants.
- Give him feedback whenever he tries something new.
- Encourage him to try more and more responsible or difficult tasks without pushing him beyond his own level of competence and aspiration. (No one enjoys being unsuccessful.)

Leadership is everybody's business, but within this concept, motivation belongs to the individual to use as he or she chooses, to move him or her among an amazing array of alternatives.

The Relationship Between Apathy and Motivation

Apathy is the opposite of motivation. It has been defined by one "wise old owl" as "apathitis: a disease of the ear and mouth caused by the other guy talking too much and you having to listen too much; it is an overdose of oral bombardment on the ear; no one ever got apathitis through his mouth, only through his ear."

Understanding motivation may not be enhanced by this bird-brained definition, but it does throw some common-sense light on apathy.

What to Do About Communication

How can you get other people to understand what you tell them? This is really more than just your problem; it is everybody's problem, and it's everybody's business too, when everybody is talking and wanting to be understood at the same time.

Your task as leader is to learn to place a higher value on listening than talking and to **become the best listener you can.** If you can do it, others may follow. If you don't do it, someone else had better, or things won't improve much.

Dr. Ralph G. Nichols (1964), of the University of Minnesota and past president of the National Society for the Study of Communications (an organization chartered to make a systematic and continuing study of communication as a means to the building of more harmonious relations within groups and among individuals), has observed that of all the ways a manager has by which to come to know and accurately size up the personalities of the people in the department, listening to the individual employee is the most important. Nevertheless, says Dr. Nichols, without **training** in listening we tend to operate at a 25% level of efficiency during a 10-minute talk!

That listening is a weak link in the chain of oral communications cannot be denied. Neither can we deny the importance of listening when getting to know one another. Learning to listen takes training and practice; it doesn't happen just because you want to become better at it.

An Example of a Complete Communication Effort

Communication takes place when people **listen** to one another and try to understand what is being said as well as speak effectively and coherently. It involves two people interacting:

George: "As I see it, we can't afford **not** to invest the money to put an ad in the newspaper, otherwise we won't have a full house and will lose our shirt."

Pam: "Do I understand you to say that we **should** invest the whole $50 for a newspaper ad?"

George: "That's exactly what I think we should do."

George makes a statement, Pam paraphrases it back to George and gets confirmation. Total communication takes place. You risk the chance of not being understood when you don't give your members—everyone of them—a chance to ask questions or the opportunity to paraphrase your words to bring about understanding. Listening takes practice, good communication takes practice.

Some Activities That Will Improve Communication

There are many exercises available that can help you improve your communication skills. Some of our favorites are: **The Hollow Square** in Pfieffer and Jones; **Body Talk** from Communications/Research/Machines/Inc., Del Mar, California; **Cooperative Squares** in Krupar; and **Getting Acquainted** in Johnson, et. al. (See Bibliography.)

Take the time to look some of these up and use them. We think that once you improve the quality of your internal communications, many of your organizational problems will begin to solve themselves, or will **at least** be more easily identifiable.

CHAPTER 15

Practical Application

We trust that by now you are convinced that leadership is, indeed, everybody's business. But now that you **know** that, what are you going to **do** about it?

Among the many definitions of "learning," there is one that seems to be particularly appropriate: learning is characterized by a change in behavior. Exactly what does this mean in terms of all that you've just read about leadership? What are some of the ways you might expect to act now, that you may **not** have done before?

In Part I, we discussed the "preliminaries" of leadership: understanding leisure, the difference between joiners and members, and how to treat the impact that first impressions have on group life. Here are a few things you might want to try as a result of having learned something from Part I:

- Use a living name tag as a means of clarifying your personal values and choosing leisure groups to join.
- Help others to clarify their values by using the living name tag in a group setting.
- Identify and work more effectively with the joiners and members in your organization, with the knowledge that the

two are different and therefore require different kinds of group experiences.

- Become aware of the dynamics of forming and perpetuating first impressions; avoid stereotyping and generalizing; be more sensitive in your dealings with new members of your organization.
- Alleviate some of the interpersonal barriers that exist among new and continuing group members by using getting-acquainted exercises as often as necessary throughout the year.
- Establish special programs for new members (big-little brother-sister orientation programs) that will bring people smoothly and caringly into the mainstream of your organization's life.

These are all things you can do to humanize group processes—**if** you've really learned something about the preliminaries of leadership. You **can**, but will you?

What about Part II? What behaviors will you exhibit if you really care about flexible and productive leadership?

- You'll be confident about running a standard business meeting, and will know how to add variety to meetings by using small-group and buzz-group techniques.
- You'll be able to set goals and to write objectives, using techniques that will encourage high membership participation and lasting commitment.
- You'll make quality decisions about major issues **before** crises arise.
- You'll use new methods of nomination and election that will bring the most qualified and interested members into positions of leadership within your organization.
- You'll make smooth transitions between incoming and outgoing officers and you **won't** depend on the typical "inside shuffle" as a means of transferring important organizational records and information.
- You'll effectively bridge the gap between meetings by using effective and efficient methods of committee selection and instruction.
- You'll work with your executive committee in the transaction of basic organizational business.

- You'll be receptive to all kinds of evaluation and be aware that only through careful participatory evaluation can real and lasting organizational changes be made.

Can you do all these things? **Will** you do them? Have you learned ("changed")?

It might be more difficult for you to apply the information in Part III, but all of these concepts do have practical application. If you've read well and carefully, here's what you can expect to do:

- Be more aware of the relationship between the need for individual fulfillment and the responsiveness and sensitivity of the organization. Use this knowledge to attract new members and to keep continuing members involved.
- Be familiar with the five basic styles of leadership; be more aware of what **your** style might be and how it affects group processes; strive to be flexible enough to use different styles to meet the demands of changing group situations.
- Be able to identify role conflict, face it and work constructively to mediate it. Clarify roles among organizational leaders and members **before** such destructive conflict arises.
- Be knowledgeable about the concepts and dynamics of interpersonal and organizational communication. Use communication exercises to highlight the importance of effective communication to group understanding.
- Be familiar with motivation—what it is, where it originates—and use this information in such a way that members will grow in their commitment to and appreciation of the group.

If you really **understand** what you have found in Part III, you'll be ready to try all these things. Are you?

The point of this final chapter should be obvious by now: intellectually knowing the facts of quality leadership is helpful, but not nearly enough. If you want things to get better, you have to **do** something with your knowledge—use it to improve group processes and to foster individual satisfaction and organizational productivity. Learning is not passive, it's **active**, and knowing without doing doesn't contribute anything to making things better. The quality of individual leadership can have great impact on the millions of people who give freely of their time and energy to the thousands of volunteer organizations now in existence throughout the world. It may not be easy to bring about organizational change, but it **is** possible, especially if you'll share what you've learned with others, trust them, and actively involve them in the process of change itself.

Learning is characterized by a change in behavior . . . what **you** do now will show what **you** have learned.

It's been a delightful and growing experience for the three of us to have written **Leadership is Everybody's Business**.

We have enjoyed writing it because we believe in what we have written. Our studies, our collaboration with others who care about the volunteer way of life, and our own personal experiences with lots of people who are involved in volunteer work have made this book inevitable.

In a very real sense, you and we now have shared something in common. Our hope is that you will want to continue the relationship with some feedback and further communication. We hope that you'll think of us as more than just three authors of a book; think of us, rather, as three people who have tried to communicate about a topic that means a lot to you, as it does to us.

Have you listened?
Have we helped?

Let us know.

SELECTED ANNOTATED BIBLIOGRAPHY

1. Alberti, Robert E. and Emmons, Michael L. *Your Perfect Right: A Guide to Assertive Behavior.* San Luis Obispo, CA: Impact Publishers, Inc., 1978. (Third Edition) A basic guide to the development of assertive behavior; extensively used in counseling groups. Many examples of communication in group and individual situations.

2. Albertson, D. Richard and Mannan, Cecil J. *Twenty Exercises for the Classroom.* Although written for classroom teachers, these exercises have unlimited application for groups of all ages when a high level of participation is desired. Included in the packet are such topics as brainstorming, listening, role playing, consensus, problem-solving and communication.

3. Benne, K. D. and Muntyan, B. *Human Relations in Curriculum Change.* New York: Dryden Press, 1951. A classic reference on the human factor in bringing about change in an organization. Over forty articles by established authorities on groups and group methods in decision making and helping groups to improve their operation. Good section on democratic ethics and management of change.

4. Blake, R. R. and Mouton, J. S. *The Managerial Grid.* Houston: Gulf Publishing Company, 1964. An instructive presentation of key leadership styles found in all groups. Based upon the degree of one's concern about the task versus the degree of one's concern about individuals in the group. It can be read for self-assessment, organization development and team-building.

5. Cartwright, Dorwin and Zander, Alvin. *Group Dynamics: Research and Theory.* New York: Harper and Row, Publishers, 1968. A must book for anyone serious about research findings and theory of group dynamics. Contents include groups and group membership, pressures to uniformity, power and influence, leadership, motivation and structural properties of groups. Thirty-four chapters by well known authorities comprise a valuable reference.

6. Fox, Robert S., Lippitt, Ronald, and Schindler-Rainman, Eva. *Toward a Human Society: Images of Potentiality.* NTL-Learning Resources Corporation, 1973. Influenced by Maslow and Lewin, the authors have developed a positive, group participatory approach to establishing goals and achieving them. Six different approaches based on a common philosophy are presented to meet the specific needs of all groups.

7. Gibb, Jack R. Dynamics of leadership, from *The Search for Leaders*, G. Kerry Smith, Editor. American Association for Higher Education, 1967. An excellent explanation of two styles of leadership: one based on the premise that people perform best under leaders who set goals, inspire people and coordinate resources; the other springing from the assumption that people develop, produce, and learn best when they set their own goals and have a wide range of freedom in directing their energies. A cogent paper that every student of leadership behavior should study.

8. Gulley, H. E. *Discussion, Conference, and Group Process.* New York: Holt, Rinehart, and Winston, 1964. Basic theory of groups and how they operate, kinds of discussion situations and questions, communicative interaction, discussion attitude and discussion leadership. Excellent sections on leadership functions, and special problems of public discussion and large groups.

9. Haiman, F. S. *Group Leadership and Democratic Action.* Boston: The Riverside Press Cambridge, 1951. A very good book on what the concept of democracy is all about in everyday groups. Includes both the basic tenets of democracy, and the practical techniques of dealing with group situations that individual freedom creates. Use as text or reference for anyone seeking both techniques and understanding.

10. Hall, D. M. *Dynamics of Group Action.* Danville: The Interstate, 1960. Relates theory with action systems which emphasize the task, the individual, the group and the community. Practical application material covers problem-solving, team-building, officer development, member participation and evaluation.

11. Herzberg, Frederick. Motivation-hygiene profiles: pinpointing what ails the organization. *Organizational Dynamics*, Autumn 1974. Pgs. 18-29. A diagnostic approach to determining the state of health of an organization. Is your organization running a fever? Showing signs of tension and pressure? Going into shock? Six profiles are given which represent the most common attitude problems found in organizations.

12. Johnson, Kenneth G., et. al. *Nothing Never Happens.* Beverly Hills: Glencoe Press, 1974. A valuable idea book for getting people involved in both content-oriented and person-oriented exercises. Although written primarily for teachers, it has potential for groups of all kinds. Main sections include getting acquainted, semantics in action, group interaction and leadership, orientations, and encounters.

13. Krupar, Karen R. *Communication Games.* New York: The Free Press, 1973. Two volumes: Participant's Manual and Instructor's Manual. Thirty-three communication games in categories of self-awareness, verbal communication, nonverbal communication, listening, decision-making, small groups, organizations and cultural communications. Basically written for teachers but the exercises can be useful in many groups for recreation as well as for improving communication skills.

14. McGregor, D. *The Human Side of Enterprise.* New York: McGraw-Hill, 1960. A classic reference for the manager-leader who wants to maximize the utilization of human potential in a group. His ''Y'' theory assumes positive characteristics in people and the integration of individual and organizational goals. Excellent section on the development of manager-leader talent.

15. Miles, M. B. *Learning to Work in Groups.* New York: Teachers College, Columbia University, 1959. A practical, self-training approach to developing one's understanding and competencies in working with groups. On the processes of small, task-oriented groups and how groups can become more effective through training. Good material on the training situation, training activities, the role of the trainer and evaluation.

16. Nichols, Ralph G. *Effective Listening*. Rochester, New York: Xerox Corporation, 1964. Four tape recordings describing important dimensions of listening, its effect upon relationships, and how to improve listening and communication skills.

17. Pfeiffer, J. William and Jones, John E. *The Annual Handbook for Group Facilitators*. La Jolla: University Associates, 1972 and annually. A loose-leaf binder of theoretical and practical suggestions for the use of structured experiences as well as directions for immediate applications. Written by practitioners for practitioners. Includes sections on structured exercises, instrumentation, brief lectures, theory and practice, and resources.

18. Russell, G. H. and Black, Kenneth Jr. *Human Behavior in Business*. New Jersey: Prentice-Hall, 1972. Excerpts reprinted in Notes and Queries, Department 224, Connecticut General Life Insurance Company, Connecticut, 06115. How to motivate is presented in a simple, practical style which centers on personal intention, perceptions and the desire to be understood.

19. Stogdill, R. M. *Individual Behavior and Group Achievement*. New York: Oxford University Press, 1959. A scholarly presentation of organizational theory with supportive research. Instructor's material on group structure, role responsibility and authority, role sanction and legitimation, role conflict, productivity and morale.

20. Sturgis, Alice F. *Learning Parliamentary Procedure*. New York: McGraw-Hill, 1953. A valuable reference for the leader who wants to learn the reasoning and fundamental principles underlying parliamentary action. It goes beyond the "*how*-to-do-it" level for those who want to know "why". Based upon the *Sturgis Standard Code of Parliamentary Procedure*, a manual of rules adopted by a growing number of organizations.

21. Sutherland, Sidney S. *When You Preside*. Danville, Illinois: The Interstate Printers and Publishers, Inc., 1964. A friendly little book for people in charge of meetings. It includes a bag of tricks about how to: get people acquainted, use the buzz session, present problems, lead group thinking, use the brainstorming session, get and keep people interested, introduce a speaker and many more.

22. Y.M.C.A. *Training Volunteer Leaders*. Young Men's Christian Associations, 291 Broadway, New York, New York, 10007, 1974. A loose-leaf binder prepared for group leaders who have been designated by the organization but are not members or elected officers of the group. Included are chapters on group leader functions and competencies, creating a climate for learning, diagnosing learning needs, helping the group get organized, helping members to be more effective, helping the group develop its program, etc.

Notes

Notes

Notes

Notes

We hope you have enjoyed reading this book. For more books with "IMPACT" we invite you to order the following titles...

THE COUPLE'S JOURNEY:
Intimacy as a Path to Wholeness
by Susan M. Campbell, Ph.D.

Five stages through which every relationship must grow ...Romance... Power...Stability ...Commitment.. .Co-Creation. The book provides a sense of perspective, of hope, of universality. It is a useful tool for evaluating and renewing the couple relationship. Incorporates activities designed to be used by couples in facilitating their own growth. Paper, $5.95.

REBUILDING:
When Your Relationship Ends
by Bruce Fisher, Ed.D.

A practical, no-nonsense book with explicit directions for working through the emotional and social steps to complete the divorce or loss of love. Dr. Fisher shows that these stages are **natural** and **necessary** to the ending of a relationship. The stages are given as fifteen **rebuilding** steps, and are keys to the successful recovery process. Paper, $5.95.

PLAYFAIR: Everybody's Guide to Non-Competitive Play
by Matt Weinstein, M.E. and Joel Goodman, M.Ed.

PLAYFAIR is a delightful excuse to have more fun!!! Detailed plans for simple and complex games for everyone. The emphasis here is on FUN, not winning. PLAYFAIR is fun to read, fun to use, and more fun to share. A valuable resource for teachers, human service professionals, group leaders, churches, and party planners. Paper, $8.95 t.

ASSERTIVENESS: INNOVATIONS, APPLICATIONS, ISSUES
Edited by Robert E. Alberti, Ph.D.

State-of-the-art papers written for the practitioner. Discusses innovations in techniques, applications in the field, and issues of ethics in the practice of assertive behavior training. Over 30 prominent AT professionals have contributed to this important reference. Hardcover, $12.95.

ASSERTIVE BLACK...PUZZLED WHITE
by Donald K. Cheek, Ph.D.

Examines the uniqueness of the black experience in America and its critically important implications for the concept of "assertion." Examples for black application of assertiveness training are presented along with practical tools and a step-by-step foundation for those who want to counsel blacks more effectively. Hardcover, $8.95; paper, $4.95.

LEADERSHIP IS EVERYBODY'S BUSINESS
by John Lawson, Ed.D., Leslie Griffin, & Franklyn Donant

Belongs next to Robert's Rules of Order in every bookstore, library, and leader's desk! Filled with practical help for the new club member, aspiring officer, and overloaded leader. Effective methods to conduct meetings, create agendas, prepare minutes, develop effective committees, and overcome apathy and hesitation. Hardcover, $8.95; paper, $5.95.

HOW TO ORDER:

Payment must accompany order, or charge to: Master Charge or Bank Americard (VISA).

Charge orders must include card #, expiration date, and your signature.

Shipping: $.75 first copy
$.15 additional copies
CA residents add 6% sales tax.

Mutiple copy discount: 10 - 49 copies: 10%
50 or more copies: 20%

Prices effective January 1, 1980, and are subject to change without notice. Write for updated free catalog after September, 1980. (Or call: (805) 543-5911.)

Mail your order to:

IMPACT PUBLISHERS, INC.
Department AI
P.O. Box 1094
San Luis Obispo, California 93406

*Don't forget your complete name, address, and ZIP!

The best in personal development...

TRUST YOURSELF!
You Have The Power
by Dr. Tony Larsen

"...this book can't make you do anything." Yet Dr. Larsen demonstrates how each of us has the power to handle "our world"—if we choose to do so. Proven personal development techniques written in a style as readable as the daily paper! Drawing from many disciplines (assertiveness to Zen) he provides readers the opportunity to learn to trust themselves, recognize their inherent powers, and make desired changes in their circumstances. Paper, $4.95.

A LIBERATING VISION:
Politics for Growing Humans
by John Vasconcellos

California Assemblyman John Vasconcellos has a vision, and he invites all of us to share it with him. Vasconcellos views our human nature as "*good*, not evil; *innocent*, not guilty; *trustworthy*, not deceitful." "...*implications for a most important direction—namely the bridges between politics and human beings.*" —Virginia Satir Paper, $6.95.

THE INNER SOURCE:
A Guide to Meditative Therapy
by Michael L. Emmons, Ph.D.

Emmons' controversial new book offers a completely natural approach to holistic health and personal development; and describes, for laypersons and therapists, the steps necessary for the reader to experience the Inner Source through Meditative Therapy. The Inner Source within each of us is a powerful ally, friend, and source of healing and creativity. Hardcover, $10.95; Paper, $6.95.

YOUR PERFECT RIGHT:
A Guide to Assertive Behavior
by Robert E. Alberti, Ph.D. and
    Michael L. Emmons, Ph.D.

This is the book that started it all! Now over 300,000 copies in print, YOUR PERFECT RIGHT has helped thousands of individuals to assert themselves. The revised and expanded third edition provides the newest information on procedures and techniques in assertiveness training. Hardcover. $6.95*; Paper $4.95.

*$7.95 effective 3/1/80

THE ASSERTIVE WOMAN
by Stanlee Phelps, M.S.W., and
    Nancy Austin, M.B.A.

The first book written by women for women on the subject of developing assertive behavior. Complete with the Original AQ Test, lifestyle chart, checklists, resources, examples and exercises that really work. Widely quoted and extremely popular with women's consciousness-raising groups, workshops and seminars. Paper, $4.95.

SURVIVING WITH KIDS:
A Lifeline for Overwhelmed Parents
by Wayne Bartz, Ph.D., and
    Richard Rasor, Ed.D.

At last! A jargon-free practical book for parents! Presents 30 proven principles of behavior applied to parent-child interaction. Clearly written and delightfully illustrated with cartoon-style examples of everyday "problem" situations, the book provides a solid guide for improving parent-child relations. Paperback, $3.95. (Excellent as a referral resource for clients.)

LIKING MYSELF
by Pat Palmer, Ed.D.

A child-size introduction to concepts of feelings, self-esteem, and assertiveness. Written for the young reader (ages 5-9), LIKING MYSELF can also be used by parents and teachers to help children learn and appreciate the good things about themselves, their feelings, and their behavior. Completely illustrated and handlettered. Paper, $3.95; with teacher's guide, $4.95.

THE MOUSE, THE MONSTER & ME!
Assertiveness for Young People (8 +)
by Pat Palmer, Ed.D.

This delightfully illustrated and handlettered book offers young persons an opportunity to develop a sense of personal rights and responsibilities, to become appropriately assertive, and to gain a greater sense of self-worth. Paper, $3.95; with teacher's guide, $4.95.

PARENTS ARE TO BE SEEN AND HEARD: Assertiveness in Educational Planning for Handicapped Children
by Geraldine Markel, Ph.D. and
    Judith Greenbaum

This guide assists the parents in dealing with various professionals in the planning of an adequate and appropriate educational program for their children. Includes examples of typical problems which arise in the relationship between parent and professional. Supportive and specific in its self-guided program for growth in parent assertiveness. Illustrated with over 30 photographs. Paper, $6.95.

Impact ✺ Publishers